James Liddy

ON IRISH LITERATURE AND IDENTITIES

Eamonn Wall
EDITOR

James Liddy

ON IRISH LITERATURE AND IDENTITIES

ARLEN
HOUSE

On Irish Literature and Identities

is published in 2013 by
ARLEN HOUSE
42 Grange Abbey Road
Baldoyle
Dublin 13
Ireland
Phone/Fax: 353 86 8207617
Email: arlenhouse@gmail.com
arlenhouse.blogspot.com

Distributed internationally by
SYRACUSE UNIVERSITY PRESS
621 Skytop Road, Suite 110
Syracuse, NY 13244–5290
Phone: 315–443–5534/Fax: 315–443–5545
Email: supress@syr.edu

ISBN 978–1–85132–051–6, paperback
ISBN 978–1–85132–061–5, hardback

Typesetting ¦ Arlen House
Printing ¦ Brunswick Press
Cover artwork ¦ Pat Melia

CONTENTS

Acknowledgements and Editorial Methodology

I am very grateful to the following individuals and institutions that provided support and encouragement for this collection: Alan Hayes of Arlen House invited me to collect and edit these essays and has provided continued enthusiasm for the project. Jim Chapson encouraged me from the outset and provided me with a list of James Liddy's publications and this gift made hunting down copies of the articles and essays a much easier task than anticipated. Though few of the essays were available in digital form, the list that Jim Chapson provided made it possible to access many of them via inter-library loan.

Tom Roedel of the Faculty Resource Center at the University of Missouri-St. Louis converted many of the PDFs that I had received via inter-library loan into Microsoft Word documents and scanned essays from journals and magazines. Those essays that did not lend themselves to conversion or scanning, I typed myself and I found this task an excellent way of exploring James Liddy's elegant prose style and unique thought progression. Jim Chapson also hunted down hard copies of some essays that I could not locate elsewhere. I am also grateful to Dr Nora Liddy for her encouragement and for providing materials. Thanks are also due to Gerard Smyth who provided encouragement, information, and access to his own files

The Thomas Jefferson Library at the University of Missouri-St. Louis was also most helpful; in addition to providing me with a warm and inviting place to work, the library's staff were able to locate PDF copies of many of the essays that appear in this volume. Aaron Lisec, senior research specialist, Special Collections Research Center, Morris Library, Southern Illinois University-Carbondale, helped in the search for hard-to-locate items.

I thank my family in the USA and Ireland for their support for this project. Thanks also to the editors of the journals where these essays were originally published. A final thanks to my superiors at the University of Missouri-St. Louis for their support: Dr. Richard Cook, chair of the English Department, and Dr. Joel Glassman, director of the Center for International Studies.

Mention must be made of three Irish-American editors who admired James Liddy's work and frequently opened their pages to his essays: Thomas Dillon Redshaw, James Silas Rogers, and David Gardiner. Redshaw was editor of *Eire-Ireland* and *New Hibernia Review*; Rogers succeeded Redshaw as editor at *New Hibernia Review*; Gardiner was the founder and editor of *An Sionnach*. Like many of us living in the American Midwest, they heard early versions of these essays delivered as ACIS conference papers. All three did much to support James Liddy's work as a critic; of course, they must also have been pleased to have been able to include his work in their respective journals. In Ireland, the late Caroline Walsh and Gerard Smyth of *The Irish Times* were great enthusiasts for his work in the essay genre.

In addition to the work published here, other examples of James Liddy's critical writings that are not included in this volume are worth noting. Not all of his conference papers were revised for publication and I have not included these in this volume. In addition, James Liddy gave many lectures to community groups in Milwaukee and elsewhere as part of outreach activities performed as a professor at UW-Milwaukee: these are not included here. Also omitted are brief entries written for literary encyclopedias. Throughout his career, James Liddy reviewed books for newspapers and journals in Ireland and the United States and these are not included here.

I have confined my selection to work conceived and revised for journal publication. A future volume of prose might include short occasional prose, reviews, unrevised conference papers, prefaces, and a selection of the amazingly inventive, bizarre, and usually hilarious biographical notes he composed for *Arena, The Gorey Detail*, and *The Blue Canary*. To avoid duplication, I have omitted two essays: *Homage to*

Patrick Kavanagh (New Writers' Press, 1971) and 'Contemporary Voices from Northern Ireland' (from Blanche M. Touhill (ed.), *Varieties of Ireland: Varieties of Irish-America.* St. Louis: University of Missouri-St. Louis, 1976). As I sought to shape this book, I kept in mind Thom Gunn's *Shelf Life*: *Essays, Memoirs and an Interview,* the non-fiction of a poet with whom James Liddy had much in common.

– Eamonn Wall

Eamonn Wall

INTRODUCTION

In his introduction to *This Was Arena*, the reissue of the literary journal he had edited from 1963–1965, James Liddy (1934–2008) recalls:

> I came to conscious life in the fifties when my luck shone in the fact that I existed in the last decade of the old life where the gods, in the recognizable shape of artists, walked the café floor and masterpieces were still made. I made my own contribution to the sixties, that earth-shaking transition in which the mountain turned into a million mice and lo a million guitars crushed poetry into the university. Made it early, from 1963–65!(5)

Though it was edited from Liddy's childhood home in Coolgreany, Co Wexford, *Arena* was a journal with an urban focus. Dublin, which James Liddy had frequented as a child with his parents and sister Nora, where they stayed in the best hotels and dined in the superior restaurants, had from the outset caught his attention and sparked his imagination. This aspect of his engagement with Dublin is brought to life in this volume in his essays on George Moore and the Shelbourne Hotel. In the early 1950s, Liddy came to the city to study at UCD where he was awarded BA and MA degrees in English. From UCD he went on to the King's Inns where he was called to the Bar in 1961.

Though it makes great swerves and has multiple frames of reference, *On Irish Literature and Identities* is framed by

James Liddy's intense and enduring attachment to Dublin and the writers who have written about it. As a writer who was formed by Dublin, Liddy reverently, and not always so reverently, follows the footprints left by those who have gone before him, walked beside him, and come after him. Even when he is looking beyond Dublin, as is the case in his essays on poets from the North of Ireland, he writes from a perspective heavily shaded by Dublin opinion. He had, after all, come 'to conscious life' in Dublin and owed it some degree of allegiance. But the sixties in Dublin, even for James Liddy, did not last forever, though he progressed to an even more momentous version of the decade when he arrived in San Francisco in 1967 to begin his American life.

It was while he was a student that James Liddy began to engage with Dublin's literary and bohemian culture. As he reveals in these essays, meeting Patrick Kavanagh was the singular event that changed his life; not only did it make him decide to become a poet, but it also over a period pushed him away from a legal career so that his full attention could be given to writing, letters, and the life of the poet. His earliest book was *Esau, My Kingdom for a Drink,* a short monograph on Joyce published by The Dolmen Press in 1962, and this was followed by two collections of original poetry from The Dolmen Press: *In a Blue Smoke* (1964) and *Blue Mountain* (1968). *Arena,* co-edited with Liam O'Connor and Michael Hartnett, ran for four issues, though the last was a double issue, gathered work from writers active in Dublin at the time, though it also reached across the Irish Sea and Atlantic Ocean, and makes for remarkable reading. Here, one will find alongside late work by Kavanagh and Clarke, poems and prose by new writers setting out on their careers: Derek Mahon, Paul Durcan, Christy Brown, John McGahern, Macdara Woods, Michael Smith, James Plunkett, Leland Bardwell, and others, as well as work by Liddy's contemporaries such as Thomas Kinsella, Anthony Cronin, Pearse Hutchinson, and John Montague. Writers from overseas include Robert Graves, Edward Dahlberg, Anthony Kerrigan, Knute Skinner and Thomas McGonigle. Living in Dublin, editing *Arena,* and being published by The Dolmen Press placed Liddy at the centre of the city's literary life.

Though we might be inclined to think of the early and mid decades of the twentieth century as being dull and repressed in Ireland, this view, with regard to Dublin and its moneyed and bohemian classes, is open to debate. Writing of Patrick Kavanagh's Dublin, Antoinette Quinn provides an opposite view:

> In the aftermath of the war Dublin was inundated with overseas visitors. War-weary English, Europeans and American servicemen, tired of rationing and food shortages, poured into the capital to dine on steaks at the Dolphin, the Royal Hibernian and the Shelbourne or to sample Jammet's even more expensive cuisine. The city centre pubs were packed. Whiskey and Guinness flowed. The wealthy and fashionable had a choice of race courses, golf courses and yacht clubs. For those who could afford it, life was one long party ... Dublin's glamour was superficial, however, and its wealth narrowly distributed. There was chronic unemployment and widespread poverty, with the jobless eking out an existence on State assistance of £1 a week (228–29).

In something that must surely have amounted to a parent's worst nightmare, James Liddy wandered the short distance from Earlsfort Terrace to Harry Street to seek his place among Dublin's bohemian literati in McDaid's. For sure, anyone looking for diversion and entertainment, with some money in his pocket, would locate much of what was required in Dublin's city centre. Of course, much of this phase of Ireland's literary culture has now passed into mythology.

That James Liddy found the bohemian/literary life to his liking is an understatement. Casting his old life aside, he entered the fray. Anthony Cronin has brought to life the setting and range of patrons found in McDaid's in *Dead as Doornails*:

> McDaid's is in Harry Street, off Grafton Street, Dublin's main boulevard of chance and converse. It has an extraordinarily high ceiling and high, almost Gothic, windows in the front wall, with stained glass borders. The general effect is church-like or tomb-like, according to mood: indeed indigenous folklore has it that it once was a meeting-house for a resurrection sect who liked high ceilings in their places of resort because the best thing of all would be for the end of the world to come during religious service and in that case you would need room to get up steam. The type of customer who awaited the resurrection and the life to come has varied a little over the years, but in spite of rather weak-minded attempts to make it so, McDaid's was never merely a literary pub. Its strength was always in variety, of talent, class, caste and estate. The divisions between writer and non-writer, bohemian and artist, informer and revolutionary, male and female, were never rigorously enforced; and nearly everybody, gurriers included, was ready for elevation, to Parnassus, the scaffold or wherever (9).

In many of the essays in this volume, James Liddy writes about the writers he encountered during these years and brings alive a vanished world. Though this world was highly social, Liddy is interested in its literary aspect, the ways in which the literary and the social cross paths in bars, restaurants, lecture theatres, and in bookshops like Parsons on Baggot Street Bridge. He provides us with a backstage pass into The Dolmen Press so that we learn something of the dynamics of the press itself and its remarkable founder, Liam Miller.

In many respects the world he describes is one in which barriers between public and private worlds are erased. Nowadays, writers are not on display as much, except, as Liddy laments, in classrooms and lecture halls at universities, or behind lecterns at readings. The author has drifted away from the saloon's public space to the privacy of her/his study.

Though Liddy himself went on to become a professor and came to enjoy the university life, it was his wont to schedule office hours in taverns as a means of uniting the classroom with the bar, the present with the past, the formal with the casual. For him, McDaid's was a university. In such books as Anthony Cronin's *Dead as Doornails* and Eavan Boland's *Object Lessons: The Life of a Woman and the Poet in Our Time,* we are offered a counterweight to James Liddy's celebration of this period of Irish literary history and social culture, particularly with respect to the collateral damage caused to lives and talents. Liddy, however, is irrepressible seeing in the move away from bohemianism a sinister Puritanism.

From the 1960s onwards, poets from the North of Ireland have occupied a dominant position on the Irish literary map. Always sensitive to change and keen to identify innovative work – given the many roles he played as a founder, editor and promoter of literary magazines – it is hardly surprising that James Liddy should cast his trained eye on the poets from the North. In the two essays included here, ('Ulster Poets and the Catholic Muse' and 'Ulster Poets and the Protestant Muse'), he considers the work of all of the major figures – from MacNeice and Hewitt to Heaney, Montague and Mahon – though, unlike Thomas Kinsella's, Liddy's analysis of these poets' work and influence is not purely deflationary while, at the same time, displaying that element. Both essays engage with violence deeply and profoundly and ask us to consider as central to Northern writing the work of Francis Stuart and Padraic Fiacc, writers whose work might be overlooked. A similar engagement is found in Liddy's analysis of Frank McGuinness's *Carthaginians*. Leaving Ireland in 1967 to live in San Francisco – the first of many American cities where he would live before settling into Milwaukee – James

Liddy's nuanced commentary on Irish violence was influenced by living in America during the period of the Vietnam War, and these experiences allowed him bring a unique view to the writing being produced from the North of Ireland. Of course, as his essay on Thomas Kinsella and Thomas McCarthy shows, he remained fascinated by Dublin, Irish cities and towns in general, and Irish history and politics.

For all of his bohemianism, James Liddy wrote his essays in a very orderly manner. Each is serious and informed by a deep regard for literary history and a reverence for the art and craft of writing. Narrative movement, clarity of expression, and opinion are favoured over theoretical jargon so as to be better able to engage the reader of the journal or newspaper in which these essays first appeared. Here, James Liddy is communicating to us as a passionate reader of literature, as a lover of the literary life, as one who is steeped in language, and as one who has learned from the practice of writing and from living among writers what literature is, and how it works. We should also keep in mind what a hard-working and productive a writer/bohemian James Liddy was. For a man who affected such a casual air, he managed to write in his lifetime fifty books in various genres in addition to all of the poetry and prose he published in magazines, journals, and newspapers.

In addition to his published literary essays, James Liddy also delivered papers at academic conferences, many of which were later revised and lengthened for publication in journals. Many of the essays that appear in *On American Literature and Diasporas* and *On Irish Literature and Identities* were developed in this way. From 1976 onward, after he had settled into his permanent position as a professor of English at the University of Wisconsin-Milwaukee, James Liddy was a frequent speaker at American Conference for Irish Studies conferences, particularly those sponsored by the Midwest region. He delivered papers on Irish and Irish-American writers and themes, encouraged and mentored his students who presented papers, took part in poetry readings with the many other ACIS members who were also both poets and scholars.

Even though he enjoyed an exalted stature as a writer, he liked nothing better than to spend time with those starting out on their careers. By staying in touch with the young, he remained young himself, up-to-date and relevant. These Midwestern conferences also provided James Liddy with excuses, if such were needed, to go Bunburying through the American heartland, that part of America where he had made his home and was never tired of exploring. Each night, of course, he re-created something of The Bailey, McDaid's, or Grogan's in bars in such far-flung corners of the Midwest as Kansas City, Missouri; Bloomington, Illinois; Davenport, Iowa; St. Paul, Minnesota; Omaha, Nebraska; Detroit, Michigan; and other places. Cities on rivers held a particular attraction for him.

James Liddy's late night conversation was memorable, hilarious, insightful, gossipy, and frequently unprintable. At the same time, it was literary always, and revealed an intense and remarkable engagement with writing.

James Liddy was a writer every minute of his waking day, and while he slept as well one must assume. Of course, these informal and boozy literary salons went on so late that no coherent shreds could be remembered the next day. In recent decades, the literary and academic worlds had become more professionalized and less social – James Liddy swam against these currents and remained a bohemian.

Notes

Boland, Eavan. *Objects Lessons: The Life of a Woman and the Poet in Our Time* (New York: Norton, 1996).

Cronin, Anthony. *Dead as Doornails* (Dublin, The Lilliput Press, 1999).

Liddy, James. 'Introduction'. *This Was Arena* (Naas, Co. Kildare: The Malton Press, 1982).

Quinn, Antoinette. *Patrick Kavanagh: A Biography* (Dublin: Gill and Macmillan, 2001).

Other Resources

For further information on James Liddy's work, the following resources are recommended:

The James Liddy Archive at the Golda Maier Library, University of Wisconsin-Milwaukee:
http://millib.wisconsin.edu/vwebv/searchResults?searchId=3350&recPointer=50&recCount=50

Brian Arkins. *James Liddy: A Critical Study* (Galway: Arlen House, 2001).

Michael S. Begnal (ed.), *Honeysuckle, Honeyjuice: A Tribute to James Liddy* (Galway: Arlen House, 2006).

David Gardiner (ed.), *An Sionnach*. Vol. 1, No. 1, Spring 2008.

Volumes of James Liddy's poems are available from Arlen House, Salmon Poetry, and Creighton University Press.

For readers unfamiliar with his work, a good starting point is John Redmond (ed.), James Liddy: *Selected Poems* (Galway: Arlen House, 2011). This volume concludes with a short biography: 'The Complex Past the Door: A Life of James Liddy' by Tyler Farrell.

Two volumes of memoir are available from Salmon Poetry: *The Doctor's House: An Autobiography* (2004) and *The Full Shilling* (2008).

On Irish Literature and Identities

One

GEORGE MOORE'S DUBLIN

Dublin is an eternal city, a city transfixed in the movement from empire to imagination with a democratic heart. It is a city lavished on by history; self-burning with long time-wraps which lie on top of each other like earthworks. One age can be peeled away to reveal another; one set of manners is tied to a hidden drawing room. Even the casual visitor has the sensation that afternoons can be very long in Dublin, as indeterminate perhaps as hundreds of years.

As a child coming to the metropolis in the forties I had the knowledge that the streets, the shops, and the hotels had done the same business for an aeon. That city of war and aftermath pulsed with an identity that still performs for me as the essential Dublin, stretching up to the somewhat shape-changed city of today and retreating in a tide of nostalgia to the eighteenth century. What the city has developed in these centuries seems to be an active consciousness, a sort of summonable-by-writer aerial view of itself – which at the same time takes the form of a deaerating process so that in descriptions of itself the environs and centre of the city become less ethereal and more physically founded. So it was that I, a County Wexford child, discovered in his journeys to this alluring, solid place a perception and perambulating method of thought that is, was, and ever will be George Moore's Dublin. Certainly I am never allowed to forget the fairy godfather or witch doctor that stood at the first door into mythic reality – nor can I ever cease from interpreting a pattern that will reincarnate elements of such a figure. When anyone hails such a site there can be no formation of a farewell.

That I share Dublin with millions who have never walked its pavements is, however, a matter of record to everyone who reads modern literature. Dublin is known through its writers as Paris is known through its painters and the island of Bali through its dancers. Writers have given the city of Dublin to the rest of the world; each literary artist has described a different aspect of the urbs. Out of the fictive imagination each has created, alongside the real city each inhabits, a secondary city. For Swift, the central area known as the Liberties was his personal mitreless purgatory with only the relief of protest. For Joyce, the whole city was a matrix from which the significations of reality flowed. For O'Casey it became the mother-city of generous social and communal impulses. Behan revelled in the mother milk of its humanity and classless spirit.

For George Moore it was a city in which to adopt a persona and to make a raid on the next stage of the articulate. When he was a child living in Moore Hall in Mayo, it was sometimes a stopping-off place to and back from the parliamentary city of London; sometimes a holiday place, a strange and smaller London, to which he went on excursions with father and brother. As a young man of the landowning class, intensely interested in the personal aspects of a dying feudalism, Moore went alone to the city whose centre was Dublin Castle during fortune-hunting season: this was the Dublin he depicted in *A Drama in Muslin*. For Moore the established writer in his late forties whose books had been published in France, England, and the United States, the city glinted as a desert with patches of fertile soil about to be irrigated by Yeats's Literary Renaissance and Hyde's Gaelic Revival. It also shone as an arena to exhibit his observation and form. It must have struck him as an ideal site for the making of a Sacred Book, as envisaged by his friends, the Symbolists.

Dublin at the turn of the century, the Dublin of both Renaissance and Revival, was a city of slightly less than half a million people, economically dominated by brewing, biscuit-making, general industry, and the export of cattle. Architecturally, it combined fine Georgian squares, domes, and public buildings with slums. Though the earlier bucks and the later dandies had gone, it retained a raffish suburban feeling and apocalyptic airs. James Joyce wrote in a letter:

> When you remember that Dublin has been a capital for thousands of years, that it is the "second city" of the British Empire, that it is nearly three times as big as Venice, it seems strange that no artist has given it to the world.[1]

(This of course was not strictly true, but there occurs a large time gap between Swift and Joyce and Moore, the two artists who were to bring Dublin forth again). Living in Dublin was always like living in the years preceding the end of the world, with the proviso that a new city was about to be born that would not be much changed. The same crowds would flow down its streets. The twentieth-century city was, to use a native phrase, 'black with people'. An anonymous writer has described it:

> One soon gets accustomed to meeting drunks of both sexes at all hours of the day. It is not an uncommon sight to come across a woman at mid-day lying absolutely inert in the middle of the road or pathway, or clutching at an iron railway, motionless as a statue, unable to stir.[2]

The words provide a vivid illustration of the familiar 'centre of paralysis' – but the new centre was beginning to cast interesting shadows. Out at the Royal Dublin Society show grounds in Ballsbridge, Dublin citizens were parting with their shillings for the novelty of a ride in a motor car, far from 'the shores of a misted lake among a dim, half-effaced peopled'.[3]

When Moore, having moved from London, arrived in Dublin in 1901 with his furniture, paintings, and Aubusson carpet, it was for a variety of reasons. A prominent motive was to get away from the hue and cry of the Boer War; but another was the need to remake an Irish identity by joining the twin movements that were setting up prospects of a post-Parnell Ireland. One of these movements was the Literary Renaissance, then giving practical impetus to the idea of a National Theatre, an adventure that Moore believed he could help with his own experience and theatrical connections in England.

As important for the returned expatriate loomed the Gaelic Movement and the necessity for it to pass the first revival stage into an active consideration of the possibilities of a modern literature in the national language. This second cause especially attracted Moore on arrival. He had packed his bags and vacated his London apartment to come to Ireland:

> in the hope of reviving the language of the tribe that used to come down from the rim of blue hills that could be seen from the windows enclosing the plain, to invade Dublin and to be repulsed by different garrisons of the Pale.[4]

The man who arrived in Dublin in 1901 was a different Moore, a maturer figure in a more progressive Ireland than the man who had known Dublin (and was known through his Dublin associations) during the 1880s and before. Then he had seen the city through the windows of the Shelbourne, so to speak. The main character in *A Drama in Muslin*, Alice Barton, had resided there during the 1882 Castle season. The city of the Lord Lieutenant, set in the context of a seedy, second-rate colony, had then been Moore's writing ground. Around the corner from the Shelbourne, at the end of a vista, stood the epitome of provincial autocracy: 'See the pot-hatted Gigmen of the

Kildare Street Club'![5] The Shelbourne Hotel itself, founded in 1824, remodelled into its present elegance in 1866, had flourished even more in the Edwardian decade than it had in the sunset of the dear queen. Its nineteenth-century spirit looked over the Stephen's Green quarter of the south city then as it does now (the vast – for Dublin – building has been caught atmospherically in a phrase by Elizabeth Bowen, in her book on the hotel, 'Tall as a cliff but more genial ...').[6] The Green he saw from the Shelbourne was spacious for a packed city; it must have created a sense of structure and form for Moore in different parts of his career. The hotel itself must have given him his other sense (which undoubtedly Moore Hall additionally provided) of rising to style and greatness. Bowen wrote of the Shelbourne, 'It stands for grandeur'.[7] At its height during Horse Show Week and international rugby nights it glowed like a modern Tara in the local imagination. In 1901 AE obtained a house for Moore around the corner, 4 Upper Ely Place – convenient for lunch, tea, or a meeting in the hotel drawing room, dominated by the great Bossi mantlepiece. Thus the novelist walked, talked, and ate (sometimes those insufferable omelettes) in the centre of the city of both old and new residences. His newly wedded panorama, that of resident rather than visitor, consisted of hotel and close by eighteenth-century townhouses, up an impressive cul-de-sac.

The book Moore made out of his ten Irish years, 1901–1911, is partly a source book about Moore, partly about Dublin. *Hail and Farewell* lacks the detail of Joyce's better-known *Ulysses*, the wide cross-sectioning. But a certain part of the city between the Grand Canal and the Liffey could be fished from its pages, as other parts could be built from Joyce's fiction. Walking and conversation, not reading, became Moore's mode of learning about Dublin; he studied daily these streets of the upper crust and inner city. No writer – perhaps not even Joyce – has looked at the south side squares and adjoining thoroughfares with more exquisite observation. 'The rickety lodging-house appearance of Baggot Street'[8] is balanced against 'The sun sets nowhere so beautifully as it does at the end of Baggot Street'.[9] Tree-lined, a stone's throw from hotel and new domicile, the vista is one of the many in this area that Moore admired with his painter's eye. Rupert Hart-Davis remarks in his preface to *Moore's Letters to Lady Cunard*:

> Few writers have so tightly interwoven fact and fiction as George Moore did in his autobiographical works. Naturally inaccurate in detail, he would transpose dates, events, and people in any way that suited his own purpose.[10]

In the phrase, entering the Shelbourne 'as any stranger from America might',[11] he conjured up a thousand and one Irish-American nights among the German waiters that he had pictured twenty years before in *A Drama in Muslin*, standing around the winter garden on the old landing watching the debutantes go off into the Castle night. The Green is the pleasure garden of the hotel in which Moore set his memorable early encounter with Yeats. Moore already had in contemplation the Anti-Sacred Book that would attempt to desacralise the Celtic Renaissance; he watched Yeats's energy and intentness.

In the city Moore remained the Mayo-trained lover of nature; as a child he had rambled around that countryside with the jockeys and stable boys (in fact, he had roamed freely by horse and boat – the lakes were higher then – and he and brother Maurice sometimes had gone by boat as far as Cong to picnic with Willy and Oscar Wilde). To this native pastoral lore, Moore added something of the nature-worshipping of the English Romantic poets. So he was able to note, when talking with Yeats in Stephen's Green, that the leader of the Renaissance lacked in his make-up what fed and created the early Gaelic literature: springtime tree and bird. Moore's alliance with a non-city instinct, the ideological pattern in his thought of opening up to a 'garden of life', enabled him to do more than penetrate Dublin with sly side-glances. It led him towards comic values in the book he was planning.

When did Moore conceive himself to be a comic figure? When did he decide that he himself was a major element in this comedy, spiced with revenge for the ambiguous invitations of Yeats and Martyn to come over and help the cause? In Ireland the price of believing in something is trouble compensated for by a profoundly liberating sense of the comic. Moore spent his last four years in Dublin, drafting his trilogy, after the interior collapse of his idealistic hopes for a new cultural scene. He had to protect himself from the idea of uselessness. Besides, all his life Moore protested, not just for art's sake but also for protest's sake. No wonder one of the great comic melodies in *Hail and Farewell* is the refrain in which he makes himself a Protestant. Being a dissident was his major forte; Herbert Howarth uses the phrase 'crystallization of his dissidence' to describe the years 1899–1911.[12] John Eglinton (William K. Magee) estimates that the moment of comic realization, spawning the truth of the work, occurred about half way through Moore's Dublin period. Eglinton sees the voice of common sense inevitably leading this way; he suggests that Moore left Ireland in 1911 for literary reasons (what other reasons could there be for Moore?): he had become 'well established' and had exhausted his subject as far as comedy and farce were concerned.[13]

Moore achieved status (and resentment) as a writer on and about the Irish scene because he could 'take off' in his style the categories of public life. His use of direct speech, as in his account of the famous launching dinner at the Shelbourne, is uniformly brilliant. In addition to Yeats and Hyde, we are here introduced to John O'Leary, the Fenian chief and literary enthusiast of the period; T.W. Rolleston, poet and critic known for a single lyric, 'The Dead at Clonmacnoise'; T.P. Gill, editor of the lively Dublin newspaper, *The Daily Express*; Standish O'Grady, translator and adapter from the Gaelic of heroic tales; Fr. Finlay, University economist; and Sir Horace Plunkett, agrarian revolutionary.

It is only with the ladies in *Hail and Farewell* that Moore's inquisitiveness fails; apart from that which he trains on Lady Gregory, Moore's hard focus on society weakens. This is so perhaps because ladies were for him naturally part of the private life. Women he eschewed here with deliberation. *Hail and Farewell* sizzles as a celebration of men and their world; appropriate for a country where the masculine will is open.

On the other hand the novelist found great relish in feasting on the bones of male victims. He cuts up like a surgeon the brain and bodies of Gill and Fr. Finlay; he excels in insult and in demonically puffed-up half-truths. He says of Horace Plunkett that he 'fears to meet anyone with a sense of humour; he dreads laughter as a cat dreads cold water'.[14] He refers in a long carefully abusive passage to the 'soft and peaty Hyde'.[15] But these skirmishes – a smiling paying off of scores as with Joyce – are wound around an environment of a city that is presented as benign and autumnal. The city was for him an habitable image, a resort for insult as well as loneliness. He liked the mass weight of it though he personally sunk into the rich status of a 'private eye'. Of Paris, Moore had written, 'Once my youth moved through thy whiteness, O City, and its dreams lay down to dream in the freedom of thy fields'![16] The evanescent spiritual state of Dublin city life that sings to us in *Hail and Farewell* had its contrasts with what Moore had written of Paris in *Confessions of a Young Man* and *A Modern Lover* and of London in *Esther Waters*.

George Moore's Dublin days were patterned; in one respect he had the soul of a clock face. Joseph Hone declared that he had a busy social life; this may have been true earlier but soon company dwindled. John Eglinton wrote, 'He soon began to be left to himself in Dublin, with a contracted circle of intimates, of whom rather unwillingly at first I became one'.[17] Moore's civic style tended to concentrate on neighbour and landlord bashing. Dublin mocks the mocker; comic virtue is catching. Moore installed himself in 4 Upper Ely Place (which is not really Ely Place at all, but the back part of the street that leads nowhere except to a nuns' garden). This section was locked with a gate and known as Smith's buildings. Gogarty gives an account of a Saturday dinner party in Moore's house and notes the deadly quiet of the street: 'Neither vehicles nor foot passengers entered Ely Place after sundown'.[18] For a small, additional rent a garden was leased with the house; it had, according to its tenant, the largest apple tree in Ireland. Moore was particularly delighted with the chatter of washerwomen in the cottages behind Ely Place. The street was comfortably Protestant; the rector the Archbishop of Dublin referred him to after receiving his letter of conversion was the Reverend Gilbert Mahaffy, who lived at 'No. 13 Ely Place, one door from the great iron gateway that divides my little cul-de-sac from Ely Place' ...[19] Other neighbours were Sir Thornley Stoker, the surgeon with whom Moore quarrelled; Cunningham, the publican, whose suicide he chronicles in *A Story Teller's Holiday*; and Gogarty who watched Moore with deadly (and posthumous) malice from the close proximity of this box-like area.

Moore's working day had the regularity of an office job. He wrote usually from 10:30 to 4:00. The business atmosphere must have been reinforced by the choice of dictation to a secretary as the method of composition. Working through dictation and thereafter further working orally from a typed manuscript had been his practice since at least *Esther Waters*.[20] He often went for a stroll after work, perhaps like a magpie on the streets, picking up bits and pieces for his current page. Occasionally he played tennis, wearing a bowler hat. After dinner he would saunter down past the Shelbourne to the National Library in Kildare Street, to catch up with his reading and to talk about St. Paul or some other hot Gospel subject with his friend John Eglinton. On Saturdays he gave dinner to his friends, a better dinner than they were accustomed to. He held an 'evening' afterwards for his two special friends, Eglinton and AE. Basically he had one circle: the literary men such as Seumas O'Sullivan, T.W. Rolleston, Padraic Colum, Oliver Gogarty, Kuno Meyer – Synge came once. Moore, in his late Dublin period, seemed like a caged animal, intent on a subject matter – the life of his city – which remained suspicious of him. But Moore never lacked friends; he was ever gracious, gregarious, and (when he wanted to be) sweet-hearted.

Moore went out also; a favourite excursion was to Michele Esposito's house where his host played the piano recital he had given previously at the Royal Dublin Society. Esposito reflected the musical culture of Dublin at this time, as did Shaw's early music criticism. He had come from Italy some years before and taught pianoforte at the Royal Irish Academy of Music; he had attractive daughters with whom James Joyce was acquainted. In general Moore's life, however, followed the role of the artist-celibate, the consummate hermit. He could clown his loneliness effectively, but Dublin responded by going elsewhere for its fun and wit. It kissed and did not tell Moore. It is difficult to judge the long contest between Moore and the city he parried with. From some there arose a fierce reaction to his personality and ways, especially after the publication of the trilogy. Not everyone took the public episode of his conversion to the Reformed Faith as a piece of playacting; he was greatly disliked for it. To Susan Mitchell he was a 'Donnybrook Fair Irishman'.[21] Gogarty asserts, 'Pernickety was the name that described Moore'.[22] His effect was more accurately set down by Harold Acton, friend of Lady Cunard, who writes of Moore's 'snowy crest and droopy moustache, his blue marble nursery eyes and cherubic complexion ... his bubbling hot dish of a voice'.[23] These characteristics might have been counter-productive in a city in which the definition of vice is a bad pose. Dublin knew Moore was made, not mad. Joyce spoke for the city in his famous lines from 'Gas from a Burner':

> '... Written by Moore, a genuine gent
> That lived on his property's ten per cent'.[24]

As Patrick McCarthy has demonstrated in his essay in *George Moore in Perspective*,[25] between George Moore and James Joyce there were correspondences; it follows there were correspondences also between the Dublin each treated possessively in his art, even as he rejected it as a permanent address. The great presences they both hated together swim passionately into their work. Moore is more prosy about this obsession; 'Two dominant notes in my character – an original hatred of my native country, and a brutal loathing of the religion I was brought up in'.[26] The comparison is insistent between the two: each attempts to fly by the same nets, nationality and religion.

Today, Dublin is Joyce's city and, to a lesser extent, Moore's. The grandchildren of Joyce's contemporaries run the professions, politics, the colleges, the business world with the great-grandchildren of Moore's tenants. Moore's own world (to which at times he was so aloof) continues diminished in the clubs, the Royal Dublin Society events, the tea-time horsey babble in the Shelbourne. If Joyce's demonic participation in the twentieth century contrasts with Moore's faded nineteenth century baiting of it, Moore stays readable and interesting. Dublin lives as a real place in his pages; perhaps it should have been more of a 'dream city' as Moore Hall in Mayo was a 'dream house'. His power of manipulating his experience and memory becomes triumphant; looking back, Patrick Kavanagh notes, 'There has been no successful autobiography. George Moore's is good because he invented his friends'.[27]

Looking back also, Cyril Connolly sees Moore as being primarily of the school of Dublin, with Yeats, Joyce, Synge, and Stephens:

> Their aim was to discover what blend of Anglo-Irish and French would give them an explosive that would knock the pundits of London off their padded chairs. All had lived in Paris, and all had absorbed French culture.[28]

(An estimate, probably, more Anglo-Irish than that of the Anglo-Irish themselves!) Today's School of Dublin looks less to London and Paris, more to New York and San Francisco; the culture of the latter is adapted to knock the pundits of the former from their chairs. Yet re-reading Moore after many years, I come upon that word-light that revivifies a complex of first feelings, and I realize that a writer has described my home. I come upon that happiest of civilized intuitions, that someone has been there before me. I can say with Elizabeth Bowen, 'For me, who was a Dublin child, the Shelbourne remains the prototype of all large hotels ...'[29] As a child I entered its lounge, restaurant, bar, with my parents, and knew with them Fred, the last of the German waiters. The tableware was as elegant, the food as uninteresting as years before, in Moore's time: in the large lounge (no longer alas a drawing room) the mix of religion and money was becoming more Catholic than Protestant. The Bossi mantelpiece passed away with Captain Jury, and the hotel became a Forte Trust House. The writing room turned into the Horseshoe Bar, conveniently near to Government Buildings for cabinet ministers to drink double brandies in. Outside remained the Green of Moore and Yeats and Joyce and me – but was Irish pond, bush, duck, and ornamental bridge ever better captured than by Moore? Surely the day will come when his bust too will dream there; an apology for the 1923 burning of Moore Hall.

Patrick Kavanagh memorably pairs Moore and Joyce as being 'truely Irish and Catholic and European'.[30] Increasingly in the EEC Dublin has this ambience; it supplants Yeats's eighteenth-century model. The part of Dublin that seems not quite time-proof passes on, is passed over. Moore's and Joyce's city survives; I amble down their somewhat altered thoroughfares. Their art is laughter-evoking, magnificent caprice in the sense of Nabokov's question, 'Isn't all art whimsical, from Shakespeare to Joyce?'[31] Such comic spirits cannot be repressed; they will always accompany us with rain and gold whiskey, the colour of eternity.

– *from* Janet Dunleavy (ed.), *George Moore in Perspective* (New York: Barnes and Noble, 1984).

NOTES

1 Richard Ellmann, ed., *Selected Letters of James Joyce* (New York: Viking, 1975), p. 78.
2 *Dublin: Explorations and Reflections by an Englishman* (Dublin: Maunsel, 1918), p. 69.
3 George Moore, *Memoirs of My Dead Life* (London: Heinemann, 1921), p. 6.
4 George Moore, *Salve* (London: Heinemann, 1912), p. 9.
5 George Moore, *A Drama in Muslin* (London: Vizetelly, 1886), p. 159.
6 Elizabeth Bowen, The Shelbourne Hotel (New York: Knopf, 1951), p. 3.
7 Bowen, p. 10.
8 Moore, *Salve*, p. 205.
9 *Salve*, p. 206.
10 Rupert Hart-Davis, ed., *George Moore Letters 1895–1933 to Lady Cunard* (London: Hart-Davis, 1957), p. 11.
11 George Moore, *Ave* (London: Heinemann, 1911), p. 98.
12 Herbert Howarth, 'Dublin 1899–1911: The Enthusiasm of a Prodigal', in *George Moore's Mind and Art*, ed. Graham Owens (New York: Barnes & Noble, 1970), p. 90.

13 John Eglinton, 'Recollections of George Moore', in *The Man of Wax*, ed. Douglas A. Hughes (New York: New York University Press, 1971), p. 28.
14 George Moore, *Vale* (London: Heinemann, 1914), p. 207.
15 *Vale*, p. 247.
16 George Moore, *Memoirs of My Dead Life*, pp 29–30.
17 John Eglinton, *The Man of Wax*, p. 18.
18 Oliver St. John Gogarty, *It Isn't This Time of Year at All* (New York: Doubleday, 1954), p. 137.
19 Moore, *Salve*, p. 367.
20 Graham Owens, 'Melodic Line in Narrative', in *George Moore's Mind and Art*, ed. Graham Owens (New York: Barnes and Noble, 1970), p. 102.
21 Susan Mitchell, *George Moore* (Dublin: Maunsel, 1916), p. 107.
22 Oliver St. John Gogarty, *It Isn't This Time of Year at All*, p. 133.
23 Harold Acton, 'George Moore and the Cunard Family', *The London Magazine*, 5, 3, (March 1958), pp 54, 57.
24 Harry Levin, ed., *The Portable James Joyce* (New York: Viking, 1947), p. 661.
25 Patrick A. McCarthy. 'The Moore-Joyce Nexus: An Irish Literary Comedy'. Janet Egleson Dunleavy ed. *George Moore in Perspective*. Gerrards Cross, Bucks: Colin Smythe, 1983, 99–116.
26 George Moore, *Confessions of a Young Man* (Montreal and London: McGill-Queens University Press, 1972), p. 109.
27 Patrick Kavanagh, *Lapped Furrows* (New York: Peter Kavanagh Hand Press, 1969), p. 227.
28 Cyril Connolly, *Enemies of Promise* (London: Penguin, 1961), p. 42.
29 Elizabeth Bowen, *The Shelbourne Hotel*, p. 10.
30 Patrick Kavanagh, 'George Moore's Dublin', *The Irish Times*, 13 June 1965, p. v.
31 Simon Karlinsky, ed., *The Nabokov-Wilson Letters* (New York: Harper & Row, 1979), pp 330–331.

THE OLD SHELBOURNE

Grand hotels remain the monuments of the middle-and upper-class gilded age that began in the mid-nineteenth century and petered out in the 1930s, of which an aftertaste persisted until after the Second World War. By then this aristocrat-tinged medium-high culture was giving way to economic pressure and a more businesslike set of manners. I was, as a child and later, privileged to enter this world through my mother's connection with the Shelbourne Hotel.

After the war she went there from the country and sometimes stayed overnight. Before that she had lived in the hotel for a few years, and she was married from it in 1931 at Westland Row church, nearby. (This last fact has an echo of Mr. Harding in George Moore's *A Drama in Muslin)*:

> Then you don't know the famous Shelbourne Hotel! All the events of life are accomplished here. People live here and die here, and flirt here, and, I was going to say, marry here.

She told me dinner was two shillings, the charge for her room was £5 a week. There were few permanent guests; a couple she remembered staying there was Sir Thomas Grattan Esmonde and his second, American, wife. She also used to see the young Kate O'Brien with her sister.

One dressed for dinner, although the food was generally uninviting. What she recollected as remarkable was the lobster mayonnaise, whose quality she never found in any other restaurant. She said living in the Shelbourne then was quiet; the hotel did not do so very well; times were hard for people. On her wedding day she planned to have a small reception in her bedroom, but when the party got back from the church the bottles of brandy, whiskey and gin had disappeared from the table.

My early memories of the Shelbourne confirm the glittering background, the theatrical sense of stage on the lower floors and the nearly invisible parade of intrigue, reminiscent of the sumptuous accounts of the resort hotel on the Normandy coast in *Remembrance of Things Past*. The Writing Room, where the Horseshoe Bar was placed later, was perhaps reserved more for the ladies and their privacy than for salesmen writing up their orders. Guests went up a stairs at the far end of the room to a Georgian interior – initially a house not part of the hotel, 32 St. Stephen's Green, where glowed a Georgian cocktail lounge at which a Martini or a White Lady could be ordered. There one could be at peace as an American tourist.

When, as children, my sister and I entered the revolving door, past the well-known porters, the first thing we made for was the lift. It was on a pulley, which we used to play with while the strange cage was in motion. When it returned we pestered the lift man – a tubby little man in the hotel's grey-and-green uniform – with questions.

The lounge was the centre of the gorgeous establishment. In contrast to the Writing Room, which was Dresden in style – duck-egg-blue walls with plaques – the lounge was decidedly Victorian, with a frieze, flock wallpaper, a large mirror over the fireplace, the Bossi mantelpiece and another large mirror at the other end of the room, underneath which was a serving table with a white tablecloth.

The most prominent waiter was Bill, a stocky, amiable character who always remembered us, but mother's favourite was the last of the German waiters, Fred.

German waiters had long been the distinctive feature of Shelbourne culture. In *A Drama in Muslin* Moore surveys the scene of the debutantes leaving for Dublin Castle: 'On the first landing, about the winter garden, a crowd of German waiters, housemaids …' Elizabeth Bowen tells, in her history of the hotel, of their internment as enemy aliens in the First World War, a fate that was avoided in the second. There is even the rumour that Hitler's half-brother was a member of the staff for a while.

Events at Christmas, during or after the hostilities, were intense to the eye of childhood. My sister and I were carrying balloons from Brown Thomas, holding on to them carefully, as we made our way up Grafton Street to St. Stephen's Green. I lost mine to the sky outside Tyson's. Nora got through the door and into the lounge before she let go of her balloon. It sailed over the tea table and the couch to the plaster ceiling. Fred and Bill rushed out, and an apprentice waiter brought a ladder.

The lounge resumed its cups and saucers, and Mother took her Scotch while we contemplated the pot of tea and thin, delicate sandwiches. Fred stopped by and regarded me. 'That's quite a child you have there, madam'.

Then they moved to their fervent topic as Mother lamented:

> It doesn't look so good, Fred. Can Hitler be making the same mistake in a Russian winter as Napoleon?
>
> Yes, madam, we are as damn stupid as the French, but Napoleon was only a soldier. Hitler is a politician and knows what to do even in snow. And God is on his side.

Fred bowed, and Nora and I ran out to the lift.

We pulled at the rope and skipped into the cage, but it did not move.

There were more connections. Father went up to interview for a medical job in Dublin with the Appointments Commission. He spent the night at the

Shelbourne and was awoken by heavy noise. He looked out the window and watched the fire and smoke of the Luftwaffe blasting the North Strand. He ducked his head back in quickly.

Shortly afterwards Mother brought us up again to the hotel. Before she left – worried about food, not having much left on the ration cards – she begged the local creamery manager for an extra, illegal pound of butter. She had taken a room facing the Green, and she left the precious butter on the windowsill to cool. It was requisitioned by seagulls.

Mother knew society. She became very adroit at pointing out personalities using the lounge. One of the first named to me was Sir Shane Leslie, whom she said was a first cousin of Winston Churchill. He was dressed in a kilt. Mother pointed to his legs. 'I wish when they wore kilts they would wash their knees'.

The tweedy gentleman in the corner she identified as Lord Adare, 'an aide-de-camp to the last viceroy of Ireland'. She recognized James Johnson Sweeney, the New York connoisseur and art administrator, whom she had met on a transatlantic liner two days before, in Cobh. There were the perennials Robert Briscoe, in his bow tie, Tom McGreevy, sometimes in his cape, Billy Wicklow, looking Hanoverian in his blue or green tweed suit, and Leo Whelan, the painter, somewhat worse for wear.

The Shelbourne lounge was a house of history. I felt about this sacred place what Osip Mandelstam wrote about his city: 'It always seemed to me that in Petersburg something very splendid and solemn was absolutely about to happen'. But other areas of the building had played their part. In the first-floor sitting room, No. 112, the Constitution of the Irish Free State was drafted.

Mother and I, in the early 1950s, spent a night in this room. Maud Gonne had died, and Mother, on a whim, insisted on going to the funeral. She had often listened to

Gonne's oratory, and that of Charlotte Despard, on O'Connell Street. We drove from Donnybrook Church to Glasnevin through saluting gardaí at traffic lights, uncomfortably close behind the hearse.

That night there was no room at the inn, so we were escorted up to the historic chamber, where beds had been made for us. As I lay there I remembered what the Pope O'Mahony had told me about the death of John Redmond in the Shelbourne: out through his window Redmond heard the crowd cheering the procession of Constance Markievicz on her release from an English prison, and he turned his face to the wall. I wondered in what room this tragic scene had taken place.

In later years I often returned to the lounge, to meet people or to indulge in celebrations, such as the fearful and awesome nights after an international rugby match. A quick sketch of such encounters would detail having an unusual tea with Patrick Kavanagh, who commented as James Pope-Hennessy walked by: 'A woman has nothing to fear from such a man'. I stood with Liam Miller by the registration desk as Richard Ellmann checked out; I noticed the curious fact that his cheque book was printed in Irish. I had tea, too, with the Californian poet Brother Antonius, who was captivated by the sing-song voices that the pages used to announce messages in the lounge. 'The queens must really be turned on by these guys', he said.

I was often in company here, with John Ashbery, with the American-Canadian writers Stan Persky and George Stanley, or with Tom Ronan, my mother's first cousin, the London correspondent for the *New York Times*, who came over for elections.

Now we have the new. In her majestic book on the Shelbourne, Elizabeth Bowen describes her subject, on the first page, as: 'Tall as a cliff, but more genial'. May these characteristics continue to mingle.

I say my last reminiscence. In 1951 I saw a pile of Bowen's book for sale on the registration desk. A few years later I collected her in the lounge, and we walked across St. Stephen's Green to her talk to the UCD English Literary Society. She was affability tinged with restraint, like her hotel.

– from *The Irish Times Magazine* (2007)

ISLAND TRUANCIES: THE SAUNTERING OF *MERCIER AND CAMIER*

The journey of Mercier and Camier is an uncertain sauntering around the centre and southern environs of Dublin, the chief city of an island. They seem as homeless as their journey becomes meaningless; they are revealed as truants whose style of comfort keeps no comfort. One of their major activities consists of the ritualizing of possessions which are not really possessions. The first chapter of *Mercier and Camier* sets up what they do: they spend most of a day in a park or public gardens, falling from grace. Then they are expelled – and they shuffle out like our first ancestors.

Mercier and Camier can be viewed as primal types whose constant energy is transformed into a protest against all regulation. Nobodaddy is authority. The two strike the reader as half-dreaming denizens of a limbo, not as rageful and malevolent creatures of Hell like the ex-machina creatures of part 3 of the novel, the never other-reflecting Madden and Conaire. When Mercier and Camier overpower and kill a policeman in part 4, they are represented as doing it in part as moral protest and in part as self-defense. They smite the monster of the Law with the pomp and circumstance of epic heroes. Tired, perhaps, of being each other's lover, they seek as a substitute for returning to their coquette Helen (Helen of Dublin, a poor cousin of Yeats's lady Helen of Troy) a little time in a house of play. What but the authority of the State would deny to such formidable companions, whose drawing of consolation is the publicity of the public house, some minor venery in a country that does not noticeably resemble Cockaigne. Each travels on, brute and comedian at once.

It is not just the Greek and Latin epics that Beckett re-echoes with ghosts and clowns in *Mercier and Camier*. The Old Testament has magnified narrative qualities which Milton followed when he rephrased the first three chapters of Genesis in the form of a classical tale where great battles and valorous deeds lead to a fixed end. *Mercier and Camier*, like the Old Testament, begins in a garden, a garden already fallen from grace and marked by wild coition, unrestricted authoritarianism, and muddled schedules. The novel can be viewed as an equally manipulative expulsion from a garden or park of the two Dublin 'butties', to whom the moral majority ordinances are worthy of a kick in the privates. The text states explicitly the state of life-grace they fall from:

> They should have felt the better for this glow of distant days when they were young, and warm, and loved art, and mocked marriage, and did not know each other.

Where they stand now demands no explication: 'They were still in each other's arms when the rain began to fall, with quite oriental abruptness'. The movement of felix culpa, a mingling of Irish and Edenic climates. Their altered circumstances makes where they meet 'a small public garden' where dogs 'begin astraddle' and 'finish arsy-versy'. If the desire of the established classes is to regain the privacy of the Garden of Eden, then Mercier and Camier are indeed out in the cold, in the place of a primordial protest. Genesis 3:21–24 and *Paradise Lost* XII: 632–40 preserve the same drama, the same exit clash, and the subsequent tillage of the common ground. They are truants, on an island of themselves!

Truants who over the small ground 'saunter', 'stroll', take 'a little stretch', and perform 'a little motion'. Verbs that imply an almost eighteenth-century aimlessness; they can't sit still in the maze they find themselves in. This maze is centered around their casual scouring of the zones of the forbidden. While in Genesis the consumption of the fruit leads Adam and Eve to recognize their nakedness, in *Paradise Lost* it leads a good deal further (*Paradise Lost* IX: 1029–45), and in Beckett, too, the sin is sexual. Here Adam and Eve are also represented by the two dogs glued in post-coitus, who are driven out like Mercier and Camier by the angel of God or the Park Ranger. 'The ranger mounted the steps of the shelter ... The air darkened immediately and turned a deeper yellow'. Later the ranger is described: 'But as if to give himself the lie he fell on them with stick and boot and drove them cursing from the pagoda'. This refers to the dogs who become an irresistible comic parallel, not only to Adam and Eve, but to Mercier and Camier who seem unable to leave each other through friendship, love, or the convenience that first brought them together and now appears to be in danger of vanishing. The departure of the dogs was no simple process as they were 'tied together' by 'the post-coitus'. At the penultimate parting, when, after they have stayed the night in a ruined house in the Dublin mountains, Mercier chooses a road in an opposite direction to that which Camier has gone, the narrator comments, 'Unstuck at last!' The extinguishing of a joint truancy is a desperate matter based as it must be on an almost criminal sense of disobedience and alienation, especially one that is as insolent as this. The excess of rebellion associated with the wild episodes of the pair seems to possess a specific Irish accretion – I shall return to this later.

And who are Mercier and Camier, besides being petulant ghosts washed up out of Milton, Vergil, Dante, and especially the Dublin stews of the local disciple of that tradition, James Joyce? Epic heroes are dignified, handsome and virile. Mercier and Camier are not just anti-heroes, they are anti-epic heroes. Camier is described by Conaire as 'small and fat ... red face, scant hair, four chins, protruding paunch, bandy legs, beady pig eyes'. Mercier is, according to the barman, George, 'A big bony hank with a beard ... hardly able to stand, wicked expression'. One is short and fat, one is tall and gaunt, and their possessions are a woman's bicycle, a sack, a tattered raincoat, and an umbrella. These are considered the instruments of escape because they look so ineffective; they are viewed as the instruments of liberation as they are pitiful and unnecessary; they shine through the pages as the insignia of the truant – one who has spoiled himself in the midst of poverty so as to render himself more outside the social norms, whose consistency remains that of the non-materialistic clown. Vaudeville clowns perhaps, at times cardboard ones; but the pearl of their integrity is the local, unequivocal, 'No surrender'. No surrender to life, as it is endured by those who possess objects. The clown represents, traditionally, humankind at its most essential: stripped of social distinction and the code of honour: the clown is ensnared in perpetual defeat but never loses hope. Particular in eccentricities, but universal in delusions, denunciations, and affirmations, such a figure comes to attention as the old Everyman. Thus, clearly, the text transforms into Mr. Beckett's Morality Play!

At an elemental level the reader can perceive in the adventures of *Mercier and Camier* the story of what happens to newly created souls, pure and innocent, when they first enter the world and are tumbled, jostled and confused by experience, by alternating psychic currents of attraction and repulsion, by desire and fear. The flowing, ebbing disturbance – the whole series of points of action and of 'non-action', or obfuscation, in the novel – is described by Plato:

> For great as was the advancing and retiring flood which provided nourishment, the affections produced by external contact caused still greater tumult – when the body of any one met and came into collision with some external fire, or with the solid earth or the gliding waters, or was caught in the tempest borne on the air, and the motions produced by any of these impulses were carried through the body to the soul. All such motions have consequently received the general name of "sensations", which they still retain (Timaeus 43c).

All the foregoing phenomena occur literally and symbolically in the novel; but with Mercier and Camier, though they may actually walk to the end of their road or their lives (whichever comes first), there is a progression. A progression, and not merely a continuation, in the lives of the characters as they gradually abandon their past and their possessions. At the midpoint of this fiction Camier renounces his occupation, which is all we are told of his past, that of F.X. Camier, Private Investigator. He tells Mr. Conaire:

> The truth is I suddenly saw my work was over, I mean the work I am famous for, and that it was a mistake to have thought you might join me here, if only for a moment. I renew my apologies, Mr. Conaire, and bid you farewell.

Mercier has already apparently forsaken his wife and children. Now they set about abandoning the raincoat; it appears they are shedding the old self in its pockets, the remnants of the life they are leaving.

They have come to the lowest circle of hell; they have come to the anarchic climax of their truancy. They must now lead themselves somewhere else. Mercier recognizes his worthlessness in the midst of primal protest or discontent against civilization. This occurs when Camier 'deserts' Mercier to go to the pub for sandwiches:

> In the end he said, I am Mercier, alone, ill, in the cold, the wet, old half mad, no way on, no way back. He eyed briefly, with nostalgia, the ghastly sky, the hideous earth. At your age, he said. Another act. Immaterial.

A comic Lear, who has definitely left behind his daughters, unable to articulate where his repression-fed, clown-inspired, mitching will lead him. At the similar episode-moment, Mercier and Camier seem to spot that they should cease cursing their predicament; thus they must accept suffering and become the poor of the last resort, that of the spirit. Eventually all is abandoned – the sack, the raincoat, the umbrella, the bicycle – and after a night in the Dublin mountains, perhaps analogous to Dante's and Vergil's ascent of Mount Purgatory, they leave each other and go their desperate, separate ways.

When they meet again in the final chapter, a long time has passed, years perhaps, and the tone, except for Mr. Watt's explosions, is peaceful: 'Were I not without desires, said Mercier, I would buy me one of those hats, to wear on my head'. They have cursed God and yearned for extinction; earlier when Mercier dashes the umbrella to the ground, he said, 'As for thee, fuck thee'. Now Mercier and Camier do not join Mr. Watt in cursing life; in fact, they are appalled by his imprecation, 'Bugger life!' Watt had been expounding the values which the main characters had never quite got to espousing: 'One shall be born, said Watt, one is born of us, who having nothing will wish for nothing, except to be left the nothing he hath'. The protagonists may have seemed to have wanted that but their manner and style around Watt's pronouncements are now light, deft, and defensively witty, with a surprising touch of the Christian Agape. In response to the bar manager, the situation is given an odd quotation: 'Pass the sponge, said Camier, according to Saint Matthew'. Mercier and Camier have gone, as Mercier says, 'Wherever the flesh creeps least ... wherever the shit lies least thick'. They have suffered the 'pains ... that permit us to supply the deficiencies of the Redemption', and come finally, twitching their memories, to the canal, where Camier departs and Mercier sits watching the sky darken, listening to the sounds of 'human murmurs ... and the rain on the water'.

There remains another level of implication in the work. The origin of the word truant means 'beggar' or 'wandering man', and it is of Celtic origin. The latter accretions of meaning add to its special relevance to Beckett's fiction. Ireland's historicity keeps the quality of errant, idle, or misfired energies; its purposes have been blocked with tribalism, ideological civil war, and the rage to disagree. Dissenting 'touchstones', with historical overlay, occur in sequence in *Mercier and Camier*. The park, which is reminiscent, with lake and pagodas, of St. Stephen's Green (from whence comes Stephen Dedalus) is 'peacefully' called after General Saint-Ruth who planted the shining copper beech, the origin of the place. Saint-Ruth commanded James II's army at the Battle of Aughrim where, as the novel says, his head was blown off. The quality to be remarked here is that this effort of leadership resulted in defeat and early death, and it includes the irony that one of the factions in King William's army that Saint-Ruth, as a Catholic loan-general, was dealing with were Beckett's ancestors, the Huguenots. The ranger, also in uniform and heroic emblems, who patrols the grass and shelters like God the Father, represents one of the forgotten, losing sides in Irish history. He is a wounded veteran of 'the great upheaval', or Great War, when it would have been in his better interest to have taken part 'in the domestic skirmish' (the 1916 Rising or the War of Independence), from the point of view of obtaining better employment: 'The bodily danger would have been less and the benefits more certain'. This perception would have centrally related to the Beckett family's traditional understanding of the conflicts. Not so a later historical anomaly in the book, where in the bog they talk about the cross that stands too far from the roadway for its inscription to be readable:

> It was the grave of a nationalist, brought here in the night by the enemy and executed, or perhaps only the corpse brought here, to be dumped ... His name was Massee, perhaps Massey. No great store was set by him now, in patriotic circles.

This minor character, obscured in the other details of the Civil War that followed the War of Independence, is the brother of the subsequent Irish prime minister, Sean Lemass; the irony added to the apparently insignificant riddle of his name lies in the fact that Lemass was also a Huguenot name, though here in the opposite context of Catholicism and nationalism. The frequency of these under-fertilizations in Irish history must aver to the conclusion that defeat and the honour of being on the wrong side confers an absurd cachet, a gleam of the hidden powerfulness of the slide or wrong direction.

Mercier and Camier bears a strange and untypical fruitfulness in the *oeuvre* of Beckett, in which is adumbrated the idea of an almost religious progress in the individual soul, and the patina of obsolescence that bestows elegance on random adventures.

– from *The Review of Contemporary Fiction* (1987)

TWO

How We Stood With Liam Miller: The Dolmen Miscellany

The *Dolmen Miscellany of Irish Writing* (1962) manifests the genius of its publisher Liam Miller, and Miller's importance to the literature of the 1960s. Miller and the *Miscellany* can be seen as a consequence of a productive ferment in the arts of Ireland in the 1950s and 1960s. There in this period was a magic global consciousness in Ireland as elsewhere. Something brilliant and progressive shone in the Dublin air: the visits of Roethke and Berryman to the McDaid's corps of writers; the expatriate pomp of Edward Dahlberg, with his memories of Lawrence and Crane over a Leeson Street shop; Richard Ellmann in Liam Miller's company paying his bill at the Shelbourne Hotel with a check printed in Gaelic; and Sylvia Beach and Maria Jolas on deckchairs by the Sandymount tower – suspicious of the milling drinkers!

In the midst of this activity, *The Dolmen Miscellany* came on the scene to signal the emergence of the first coherent group of writers since Yeats and the Renaissance. Liam Miller designed the brooding style of the publication which, halfway between a journal and an anthology, heightened the effect of its arrival.

Liam Miller and The Dolmen Press staged a spectacular coup aimed at establishing a cluster of major new poets. The Dolmen, in effect, replenished the literary energy of the first quarter of the century. The *Miscellany* represented the climax of the first phase of The Dolmen Press where the emphasis was on the production of poetry from the Dublin locale. Once Miller had set up a central nucleus of arresting poets, he turned his attention to criticism and the Transatlantic. In this way he brought his publishing house back to Yeats and Joyce and Synge. Scholars came and went in Baggot Street like Lady Gregory's swallows. How Miller waited for them in June when the American semester was out and they arrived from the airport, how he cherished and encouraged Richard Ellmann, John Unterecker, Max Rosenthal, David Krause, and many others! Whether Miller brought out scholarship or poetry he did it in the same gorgeous, determined, way. Miller served both the new and elder Irish literature with an extraordinary range of skills and taste culled from the designs and typography of William Morris, Harry Clarke, Eric Gill, and Lilly and Lolly Yeats.

I have described Liam Miller elsewhere in the context of his friendships, and specifically of his connections with the distinguished Irish-American translator Anthony Kerrigan. Now I would like to conjure up the appearance of *The Dolmen Miscellany of Irish Writing*. I always admired the blood-red cover that is perhaps trying to become a vinous colour beloved to its creator. Looking at it, I get something of the same respect George Pompidou expressed as he held in his hands the 'insignificant small' first edition of *Les Fleurs du Mal*, at the centenary in 1957. The faint blue lines across the sombre red of the *Miscellany*'s cover suggest the shield of a new generation. The *Miscellany* possesses something of the sharp provocations of Baudelaire. The editor, John Montague, and the poetry editor, Thomas Kinsella, intended to administer a midcentury shock of proportionate magnitude. The tart brevity of the editorial allows it to be quoted in full:

> In recent years a new generation of writers has begun to emerge in Ireland, probably the most interesting since the realists of the 1930's. While not forming any sort of movement, they do reflect a general change of sensibility, and this *Miscellany* is an attempt to provide them with a platform. They are, in general, more literary than their predecessors: many of them are poets, and the prose-writers seem to be working towards a more experimental form of story. The main link between them, however, is their obvious desire to avoid the forms of "Irishism" (whether leprechaun or garrulous rebel) which have been so profitably exploited in the past. In such a context, a little solemnity may be a revolutionary gesture. We have concentrated on work of some length, or of a kind not usually represented in magazines, in the hope that, as well as providing an impetus, the *Dolmen Miscellany* will also be a record of work in progress by a generation. Future issues will, of course, depend on your support.[1]

Note the Baudelairean exhortation, 'In such a context, a little solemnity may be a revolutionary gesture'. This is Montague's call to arms; it is Parisian: to the barricades!

This is a salvo for a less localized literature and it is naturally a manifesto. It can be said that the whole *Miscellany* is a manifesto, more by sample than by direct statement. Nevertheless, the importance of the editorial can not be overstressed. The guerilla preface seems still warm: its cadence is the extension of the lyric, its clarity is the short lunge of the Irish lyric, its tartness an urge to smother the bucklepper and the keepers of hurleys and Gaelic grammars alike. Two key words – 'platform' and 'impetus' – show the constructed force of the Dolmen agenda: it reads as a flat fiat, a writing-not-talking ethic, this is 'Coole time'. The tone of the passage is contained in its assertion about a generation. The real demand is an invitation to set up a rejuvenated republic of letters inside the recently legislated into existence Republic of Ireland.

The contributors are apostolically twelve in number, all male, six Dubliners, a native of Belfast, four of rural origins – and not a Kerryman in sight – and now only two dead, not a bad record for us who followed the rule of Bohemia which seemed to impale us at the time. McDaid's was the clearing house for our notions. There, over the counter, or at the few tables, we shoved smoke stacks into the disappearing Celtic Twilight, there we listened to Paddy Kavanagh's better revolution, 'No more Wolfe Tones'. Anthony Roche comments:

> The key development in the 50s had been the emergence of Dolmen as an Irish publishing house primarily devoted to poetry ... In putting together *The Dolmen Miscellany of Irish Writing* (1962), editors John Montague and Thomas Kinsella spoke of their "obvious desire to avoid the forms of 'Irishisms' ... so profitably exploited in the past". The native freedoms bestowed by Dolmen enabled Kinsella's writing to embark on the early stages of an experimental breakdown of inherited poetic forms and a stable fixed identity. Equally, Montague was able to accumulate individual poems and volumes into his 1972 sequence *The Rough Field,* a personal odyssey exploring the ramifications of his own history in the larger history of the island and the surfacing crisis in the North. *The Rough Field* stands as testimony to Liam Miller's high production standards: the woodcuts indite woodkerne and Elizabethan soldier alike ...[2]

Who is this extraordinary figure, Liam Miller, who effected such a sea change in our literary culture? He was both a new kind of impresario and a reinventor of prevailing tradition. Miller seems to me a sort of Diaghilev, for he possessed the surest touch about the networking arrangements of the Irish, English, and American literary dance, and at the same time was capable of initially breathtaking proposals. Paradoxically, there was more than a touch of Yeats about Miller. The strands of this comparison would include the magisterium of an august press name coupled with a basement image of an arts-and-crafts operation, the rigid fascination of both men with the theatre that indulged both pragmatic and theoretical inclinations, and a presentation of mother Éire filtered into the golden, indeterminate performance of postliberation –

in other words, just the right mix of the colonial and the postcolonial. There are dissimilarities between these Svengalis: notably the replacement of Rosicrucianism with Romanism, the occult by the tavern.

Liam Miller accomplished a new phase in Irish writing without in any way caring to be a writer of poetry. He was a keen critical writer on Yeats, as my own students attest in their research papers on the great poet. There has been talk of the 'dominance' of the Cuala and Dolmen presses in Irish literary history, but there remain large exceptions to this. For instance, Dolmen had little to do with the intense interest in Patrick Kavanagh. I stood on Baggot Street Bridge with Miller and Kavanagh while the former took photographs for *Self-Portrait*, the printing of the RTÉ essay, which was the sole publication of a Kavanagh work by The Dolmen. On that occasion, Kavanagh was cheered by the architectural students on the roof of the just-completed Bord Fáilte building – the king in his own kingdom. Kavanagh was the only major poet of that era to survive without an Irish publisher and to get by on the London connection. This freed Miller's energies to look after the latter career of Austin Clarke and the generation of Kinsella and Montague. Between 1955 and 1975 Miller ran Irish poetry almost unchallenged.

Kavanagh, however, had a substantial influence, or side effect, on the *Miscellany*. His presence floats through the poems in the volume and is most visible in the contributions of John Jordan. McDaid's is the scene of Jordan's story 'First Draft', and the Monaghan poet is often invoked in the 'Poetry Chronicle'. An example is Jordan's comment on the Beckett-named poem of Montague's, 'Murphy in Manchester':

> These lines of course reveal one of Montague's weaknesses, his tendency to graft on to his observed people an expected response encountered before in literature. Murphy is not Mr. Patrick Kavanagh and to suggest that he is, even fleetingly, is sentimental (DM 112).

Our beacon publication was structured well by its editor: the contents of the *Miscellany* are exquisitely framed at either end by two carved pieces of prose by the mid-elders, Brian Moore and James Plunkett. The poetry may be more uneven than the fiction; on a rereading one is struck, however, by the poems that remain vivid. Kinsella's 'A Country Walk' keeps its descriptive glamorous air while Pearse Hutchinson's poems surprise by their freshness and casual mastery of phrase and line. I now have the impression that Valentin Iremonger is a major poet, and he is undoubtedly Ireland's John Betjeman:

> Jane Brown had red hair that dazzled
> The boys in Sandymount when she was even eight.
> Going from school, all would be eager,
> Politely to see her to the garden gate ...

and:

> God love you, Miss Jane Brown. I had forgotten
> Your pale cheeks, your smile and your red hair,
> Our walks by Marley, our melancholy love-glances
> Our kiss on the darkened stair (DM 80–81).

Iremonger's stanzas come from the Jackeen school of nostalgia; what we have lost from adopting a republican constitution! Iremonger would have made a fine poet laureate presiding over Aosdána. Also he, not Anthony Cronin, is Auden's first Irish branch.

At the time of the *Miscellany*'s publication, I considered Montague's essay on Oliver Goldsmith's *The Deserted Village* as being out of place. Its inclusion seems either a provocative decision, or perhaps merely a personal gesture by the editor. I can but speculate: was the offering a move designed to make the *Miscellany* more variable, or was it a determination to let the reader know that up-and-coming writers were not just lyric voices recycled but also analytical thinkers? This suggests the roots of some comments by Thomas Kilroy in his 1982 essay, 'The Irish

Writer: Self and Society, 1950–80'. Kilroy remarks on 'the *Miscellany*'s criticism which seemed to promise at once, and perhaps for the first time, a native school of criticism which could command respect'. This may be another element of the 1960s, a greater international consciousness that the *Miscellany* helped bring about, though Irish writers may read Kilroy's comments as laying an undue burden on the individual poet or fiction maker. In a sense, Irish writing since then has been as globalized as Irish artists have been. Kilroy charges *The Dolmen Miscellany* with exemplifying the Irish writers' privileged status because their poetry and prose has not made 'any significant impact on the kind of life, the kind of society we have in this country'.[3] In a way, the globalization of writing has led to the least significant impact: the obvious commercialization of Irish culture for tourism, the Celtic Tiger fetishes of Joyce and Yeats. Montague's Goldsmith article now seems intended as an image of our national and moral decay in the pre-*Miscellany* days of the 1940s and 1950s. Was the ghost of Goldsmith being used to confront the de Valéra-fringed fantasies of Daniel Corkery, the Claddagh pieties of F.R. Higgins and Walter Macken?

The question of where an Irish writer belongs in his society and in the evolution of his art is a complex one, but any answer must at least partially deal with a return to near-origins. I would like to look at the *Miscellany*, and my three poems in it, in the context of my own collective past. My feeling for where I began as a poet would have to make the journey to Munster antecedents, talkers and poets, 1700–1900, who held forth in one language and then drifted to another, who had not the opportunity (except indirectly) to engage with critical prose, unlike their English counterparts. Most of them were cognizant of their colonial milieu, but they must have felt their effort lay in the delights of a charged language. Three events improved their position: the revival of the Irish language; the example of Yeats and his associates and their noble performance of their tasks; and – dare I say it – the leadership and style, the working resources and methods, of Liam Miller, who led us out of another flat period in our cultural history. Though for me the little black-and-white City Lights books from San Francisco, sprucing up the Hodges Figgis shelves, opened the necessary doors of liberation, it was Liam Miller – his availability, his power to carve niches in the public air for writers – who created space, and page, and attention to my poetry. My generation, in particular Kinsella and Montague, have been appropriately grateful.

What was it that made our nonpareil begetter march us off to the campuses of the United States, past the Blaskets and the Arans? I would like a biographer of Liam Miller to give us, in time, extensive answers to these queries. Liam Miller was my companion for quite a few years. We accumulated many pub-flier miles and astonishing encounters and conversations. I remember him at Yeats's Corcomroe Abbey with Mary Holland – we were asked in the hushed tones of Synge to leave a pub because the owners had to go to a funeral. I remember being with Miller and Kinsella at Louis MacNeice's funeral outside Belfast, and then afterwards going through groups of MacNeice's friends from the 1930s, in house and pub. I remember how, after a tiring day in the 'field', Miller would make the most wonderful, spontaneous, omelettes in his Baggot Street kitchen. Around the corner from the house, The Dolmen Press gleamed in its machines, guarded by his brother-in-law Liam Browne and a few other workers.

At either end of this Bohemian district, stood two guardhouses: on the bridge May O'Flaherty's concierged books with window displays of the latest Dolmen editions, and at the other end was Phil Ryan in his two-tiered heaven of a pub. Mine host presided over the warming of the moral of our group which could include W.R. Rodgers, James Plunkett, the sister-in-law of Brendan Behan, or Tony and Elaine Kerrigan, among others. Liam and his wife Jo would then invite us over the street to their place for after-hours food and libation. That office drawing room was full of illustrated and fine art books, and Liam always had special pleasure in talking down and showing 'round his Eric Gills.

> He will sit alone on a bench without
> the humour of a sentence out of Synge.
> He will try to whisper through shut lips
> to the beautiful pages he made on an
> endless Baggot St. summer. He will imagine
> a stage with kegs of porter like a picture book
> of wings. Go, barter twilight for the first scene.[4]

– from *New Hibernia Review* (1998)

NOTES

1 *The Dolmen Miscellany of Irish Writing,* ed. John Montague (Dublin: The Dolmen Press, 1962).

2 Anthony Roche, 'Platforms: The Journals, The Publishers', in *Irish Poetry Since Kavanagh,* ed. Theo Dorgan (Dublin: Four Courts Press, 1996), p. 73.

3 Thomas Kilroy, 'The Irish Writer: Self and Society, 1950–1980', *Irish Literature Studies,* 9, ed. Peter Connolly (Gerards Cross: Colin Smythe, 1982), pp 176, 182.

4 James Liddy, *Collected Poems* (Omaha: Creighton University Press, 1995), p. 308.

CARDS OF GRATITUDE
KAVANAGH'S LECTURE SERIES: UCD, 1956

In the packed theatre after the priestly introduction, the murmur from mouth to mouth turns on itself – the rumour to the effect that something is happening in the story of Ireland. Kavanagh, the beautiful but complex Ringmaster is back, the circus animals are docile and excited. Paddy swings to the left, where *Irish Press* journalists who have been providers for him stand along the wall; he refers to a current columnist: 'Lennox Robinson, the official Protestant to the state ...'

After long applause the circus hive explodes. Paddy in mid-swarm invites me and my sister into the Professors' Room in the corridor leading to the great hall. The academy, which had never sung for me, now warbles cantatas.

After the ball is over, in O'Dwyer's a small drear crowd. The wall dark brown with spots, lounge tables. Day glasses turn into night glasses. The painter Paddy Swift is there, a dark Prince Hallish to Kavanagh's Falstaff. I take a seat in suspicion's labyrinth, buy my round. The small hunger maybe but the last loneliness.

By the facade of Earlsfort Terrace: if the Gaels have tears, they shed them now in disappearing sunlight before the second lecture. Leo Holohan and Paddy walking in slow friends' parlay execution mode, tired of La Mancha, tired of being On the Road. Leo in his large sweater, Paddy under his hat; no rest for men.

The room for the next lecture is not the Physics Theatre but an upper room in Earlsfort Terrace. Paddy talks about Roy Campbell's Penguin translations of the poems of St. John of the Cross and uses some of the poet's language; the night is bathed in a crystal cistern, and the young poet Dickie Riordain gets into the mood and verbally pours it over himself and the audience at the end of the talk. We sit metaphorically in a river of trees of flame, phosphorescent cedars, caressed breasts, Coplas pop songs of love, and sheen of blossoms that linger in the bar afterward.

'Let there be duende and the dancing of teeth', Paddy said. 'We stammer, we have to be astonished', Paddy said. 'Ezra Pound was Longfellow's great nephew', Paddy said. He was right, we laughed.

THE LEFT BANK AT BAGGOT STREET BRIDGE: PARSONS BOOKSHOP, C. 1960

The ladies presided. Miss O'Flaherty and Miss King. Miss King was Gertrude, Miss O'Flaherty was Alice. Put it another way and more appropriately, Miss O'Flaherty was Adrienne Monnier and Miss King Sylvia Beach who owned adjacent bookshops on the Left Bank, but this was one bookshop. Replace James Joyce with Patrick Kavanagh, the Coupole café with McDaid's. Less kindly, for they were benign, some locals referred to them as Scylla and Charybdis, intimidating sirens perched by the waters of Baggot Street Bridge. Their songs took the shillings out of your pockets for words on paper.

Miss O'Flaherty was 'May', Miss King was 'Miss King'. May could be seen eating supper in Caffolla's fish-and-chip shop across the street. Miss King was never seen to eat. Not that May wanted to be seen eating there; it was not quite her image of herself. May was talkative and somewhat vain. Miss King quietly said real things, including the best gossip. May's opinions were more forthright and expressed with an emphasis on morality befitting her Limerick origin; I can still hear her comments on Terence de Vere White fleeing to London with an author who was not his wife. May kept the hearth, and Miss King, from a farm near Clifden, kindled the fire.

When I said 'O'Flaherty' to Patrick Kavanagh he replied immediately, 'Liam or May?' May was very pleased with the response when I told her. May used to say to people, 'James Liddy never did a tap of work in his life', a remark enthusiastically approved of by Kavanagh. Miss King thought maybe I did some work; she held out the possibility. She certainly took my part when needed and I stood guard by her corner of the shop, back left, where the real books were stacked. Customers went to the main counter where May dispensed light wares; writers and literati turned in the direction of Miss King who also did the special ordering. The window display was tastefully done, with recent Dolmen Press books holding prime space. Once the famed expatriate Edward Dahlberg, a friend of D.H. Lawrence, came on the premises. Looking around, he exclaimed, 'Where are the books?' He meant paperbacks are not real books. He was led gently to Miss King's corner, where hardcovers thrived.

A parade of writers and personalities came through Parsons. The business of literature, the pleasure of 'news'. Kavanagh came every morning; there was his stool in the corner where he perused free reads of the day's journals. A noggin of Scotch was sometimes provided with them. May kept a journal behind the counter in which her authors were invited to write their comment or greeting. Paddy's was vintage mysticism. Frank O'Connor came for the afternoon newspaper; May showed me his entry, which was wooden like his conversation. John Montague was Miss King's favourite, for both amiability and *douceur* of lifestyle. While anecdote reigned, on the opposite side of the room May would be defending church and state as when she protested in defense of her employees to the American O'Casey scholar David Krause that 'all my girls are virgins'.

Great events like that did happen in Parsons. May introduced Kavanagh, 'our greatest poet', to Archbishop Simms who was shepherding the visiting archbishop of Canterbury through. Simms told him that Kavanagh was 'our Swift'. Unfortunately, Paddy recognized Canterbury from television the night before, where he had been decrying the money wasted on space travel to the moon. 'Are you that old fool?' Kavanagh growled.

Sir Anthony de Haughton of Haughton Towers in Yorkshire (famous as Shakespeare's hiding place in recusant times) appeared often bedraggled, seemingly clad in a sack and carrying another one. In the RAF in the war, he had bombed his own airbase; he was now a remittance man in Dublin. He would buy a £100 worth of hardcover volumes from Miss King, some of her special books, put them in the second sack, go outside, and drop them in the Grand Canal to the horror of the ladies. They would debate whether the books would have second-hand value. Kavanagh commented, 'He should have given them to the poor'.

I miss these goddesses, one who loved writers, one who loved poets. I felt May was a prelate to whom one paid respects, while Miss King was a priest to whom one went for gentle confession. The eventual loss of Parsons in 1989 signalled the shutdown of Dublin as a literary city. The last time I saw Miss King was at Katherine Kavanagh's funeral, where she was chatting with John Montague on the other side of Rathgar Road. An article appeared in, I think, the *Sunday Tribune* on the closing; Miss King was interviewed, and displayed a postcard I had sent her from Spain. Now I send them both a large card of gratitude.

MYLES'S ODYSSEY: DUBLIN-ARKLOW-WEXFORD, 1962

Querulous about shifting absurdities or shams, Myles na gCopaleen justified the erection of sardonic masterpieces. He zoned Dublin into a desert isle disc of tomfoolery.

His newspaper column fixated on a clock that had stopped at eleven. The particular timepiece was attached to Andy Clarkin's business premises on Pearse Street. Myles wrote that time would be 'reintegrated' if those hands moved. How many generations had been baffled, or had their lives ruined, by the vagaries of public, or public house, timepieces?

Myles, relentless in noting the orphic, ran the text every time his column appeared: 'Andy Clarkin's clock is still stopped'. Was Myles getting tired? There were rumours that collaborators had been called in to his lunch headquarters, Synnotts of South King Street. He needed a holiday from his routine. Over a drink in McDaid's he'd ask the barman for a job tip; as often as not he'd go to Hodges Figgis bookshop looking for a position. He'd take each issue of *Time* magazine to the Bailey to hold up his hands in horror at the grammar and syntax.

Basil Clancy, editor of the cultural bimonthly *Hibernia*, commissioned him to do a piece on the new opera town of Wexford. Myles enjoyed the sunny Southeast, and especially Arklow, a fishing town with a Viking name. He appreciated the Old Ship, a bar favoured by fishermen who had taken up painting in retirement and spent the evening badmouthing Picasso. Myles's major port of call was Hoyne's Hotel and its Lisdoonvarna-born proprietor, Josie Callinan.

Wexford was further down the road. Clancy had prudently sent along Paddy Gallagher of RTÉ as a back-up, and Paddy brought me in as a minor back-up. We escorted the great scribbler to the Talbot Hotel. A ball of malt for Myles in the garden; deckchairs; a lovely day. We tried to link up with a poet who wore a bow tie, a customs and excise official whom I later found out locked himself behind his office door to write poems. We came back from the phone through the glass doors: Myles, our bard, had flown.

No clues as to our rara avis. We asked all over Wexford. Commodore Barry's statue knew nothing. The Bullring had nothing. The heads turning in Banville's Pub had nothing. Then, in Morrissey's auction house on the quays, we found Myles, seated in an inlaid nineteenth-century chair, murmuring 'Andy Clarkin's clock is still stopped'. He was enthroned, yellow-skinned, jaundiced, the Latin Quarter hat stuck over his eyes. I gazed on the facade of Gulliver's world. Clocks are so small they don't work, but they will have to come together. They will agree.

SCOLDINGS:
MOREHAMPTON ROAD, JANUARY 1967

Tom MacGreevy said:

James, I'll have to keep on scolding you because you're close to things essentially Irish but not part of them. I'm an old scold like Cathleen ni Houilihan. When you're seventy-three I'll put my harp aside for a moment to ask Our Lord to get some young feet to show as much thought for you as I have ...

I imagined you had decided not to bother with me because of my warning about Kathleen and The Woman of Three Cows. Your poem and note made me so happy I could begin scolding you again. You don't like the last stanza of your poem, your fears are (as my friend of the days when I was your age, Patrick Tuohy the painter, used to say) 'teetotally wrong'. You will grow to replace the elders alright. Kathleen (and our Hugh, yours and mine) and the Lord God himself will see to that ...

Maud Gonne used to say, when she tried to do something for Ireland she was protected. When self-will crept in things would go awry on her. The circumstances change the essentials don't ...

I have written over five hundred pages of autobiography in which I hope values of my small-town and country-side upbringing prove as good as anything that constituted a challenge to them afterwards. I have just demobilized myself of the Royal Regiment of Artillery (even if, on the whole, it was very kind to me) ...

Meanwhile the scoldings:

I don't see Graves as an elder to any Irishman but then I don't know him or his work. I came across Hemingway but he didn't matter to me. I read 'A Farewell to Arms' and though I thought the dialogue had point it seemed to me that the killing off of the child was quite arbitrary, being a means of bringing the tale to an end – like the suicide of the little girl in 'The Wild Duck' which I never believed in. The only other story I read was 'The Old Man and The Sea' which I thought was no more than a boring offshoot of the boring 'Typhoon' which Conrad wrote. Things Hemingway told me of his activities in the war made me think of him for all his amiability a fellow of Americanly limited understanding. I will be disappointed if you throw me away just the same.

But, dear James, we'll talk more next week and I'll scold you again. I'll have you view some Jack Yeats pictures, I have them bundled in packages around my desk ...

A Wake in Grogan's: South William Street, 1973

Grogan's was quite packed. I sat at the counter in the lounge, while from the bar came sounds of fiddles, spoons, and even at one point an old man who couldn't sing singing while all around him voices were going 'Shush!' 'Shush!' 'Shush!' I wondered were they trying to *cuineas* the crowd, or were they saying it at the old man. The artlessness of it: dreary, repetitive, and sweet.

I remarked to Tommy the barman that I hoped this was not a new resident group. 'Oh, God, no', he said:

> but it is the proper form for a regular's wake. Poor Kevin, he wouldn't have gone for it at all. I don't want music in the bar, you'd go mad having to listen to that every night. It's hard enough to keep going without that, you know. I like a place where you can talk to each other and that's what this is, we're not getting any television for the World Cup either. I don't suppose you're that fond of football yourself, no more than myself, but who wants a row of yobbers screamin' and yellin' at it and they don't know the first thing about it ...

I was here in search of Kevin's ghost. I knew it was a considerable ghost wearing a tweed cap, maybe a bow tie.

I remember as far back as McDaid days when Kevin had the antique shop in the basement of the Hibernian Hotel he would address us modestly:

> Yes, I come from Cupcake, Massachusetts, over the hill from Emily Dickinson, my family might have been her servants. If so they were excellent help. I'm sure they gave her a nice funeral.

When I came back in the summer his greeting was:

> From Milwaukee my God, I have to believe it. The city of the divine Hildegaard, the most ravishing singer in the world. War was alright if you could listen to her performing; can you envision the Embassy room of the Plaza Hotel: a Goddess of light by the piano, long white gloves 18 inches down on her arms, her white and golden dress, and GIs crowding in like it was an Army Base. Hildegaard, the queer who made Milwaukee famous.

I was home.

He died of a chest infection, whatever that vague diagnosis might mean. He knew it was coming; he used make jokes about it. He once told me he had his tux in which to be buried. People in the bar used to ask him what would happen to his ashes. 'Oh', he said under his waxed moustache over trim jutting beard, 'they can bring them into Grogan's and put them into all the ashtrays'.

Kevin used to bring into the pub letters J.D. Salinger had sent him, to show them round:

> Jerry and I were in the Battle of the Bulge together, it was pretty hot in the Ardennes at the time. He was a guy who could see things through, he could comment well under fire. You could be bursting with laughter on your last minute with a mouth and an elegance like that around. We had our breakdowns later. I never went back over there, and he locked himself up under latch and key and never let himself out.

I wonder where those letters are.

– from *New Hibernia Review* (2008)

How We Stood Our Rounds: Bohemian Dublin in the Sixties

We have Proust's word for it, backed up by Beckett, that voluntary memory does not hold a candle or a glass to the involuntary kind as a means of evocation. But for me involuntary memory is not a rare experience, as far as Dublin is concerned. We Irish are consumed with spontaneous reminiscences, and perhaps this could be the tasteless gift at the heart of our culture. Yet, there seems something occult, as well as native, in unquenchable, unforsakeable, but unbidden re-enactments of the past – *textes pour quelquechose*. 'When I grew up' is always coming to an end. I want to ask the ghost of W.B. Yeats, 'How many times have Greece and Rome died?'

For the burial of the Fifties and Sixties Dublin, I refer to a pronouncement by the art critic of *The Irish Times* on the death of the painter Patrick Collins, on 2 March 1994. Brian Fallon says of Collins, 'He also mixed easily with poets and writers generally, and was central in the now vanished Dublin bohemia which included Patrick Kavanagh and many more'. 'Now vanished', the perfect undertaker's phrase. One notices in Fallon's sentence that Kavanagh preempts other figures in the Dublin of my youth. He was, as often naively but comically narrated in his verse, the god of the scene. By the time I met him in 1956, he had transferred from the cafe to the bar. Of my friends recalled here, Kavanagh was the native-born presentation; Liam Miller fashioned the youthful succession to the elder poet; and Anthony Kerrigan was the Christopher Columbus who arrived on our shore to find the indigenous literary set he had partly imagined.

Anthony Kerrigan was the laureate translator. He put Miguel de Unamuno into English, a seven-volume *Collected Works*. He did five books of Jorge Luis Borges, fiction and poetry. He gave the English-speaking world Reinaldo Arenas's *El Central* and most importantly Camilo Jose Cela's *The Family of Pascal Duarte,* that Goyaesque portrait of minimal domesticity. Three years before his death, Kerrigan was awarded a National Endowment for the Arts senior fellowship in literature and a grant of $40,000. He was, of course, a poet in both his languages, English and Castilian; without that he could not have been a laureate translator. Not the least part of him was his manner of a postwar bohemian – apocalyptical, magnificently brazen, ready to intervene in the affairs of the great with aplomb, and disturbed, but lucidly and craftily so. I noticed the resemblance between John Berryman and Kerrigan when they joined forces, in Dublin's chaotic nights of the late Sixties, and charged. They gave no quarter, at least not to themselves. They were aficionados of Ireland – Kerrigan under the shadow of Borges, Berryman in the augury of Yeats. They felt they were among their own people, a presumption readily disputed by Patrick Kavanagh and his court. This in no way compromised the fun Kerrigan and Berryman had near the banks of the Grand Canal. Dublin is a one-poet town, and they didn't care.

Probably driven by the whimsy of being born from an Irish-sounding father in such an American-sounding place as the Canal Zone, Tony Kerrigan arrived in Dublin, where Christian Brothers-fed armies used to clash by night. He appeared with his wife Elaine at the yellow brick tower of Stephen Dedalus and walked up the winding Buck

Mulligan stairs. Zero Mostel had just been there casting Leopold Bloom's voice up the chimney. Tony, already myopically eloquent under youthfully fringed white hair, prayed at the stations of the waistcoat, the cane, and death mask. I was late that day opening the tower, delayed by the hardy business of buying poems, from Kavanagh in McDaid's, for my new magazine *Arena*. We had concluded with 'luck money' and a handshake.

I was the second – the summer – curator of Joyce's Martello Tower. It had just been opened in the great unresisted cultural flow of the Sixties. The nation was full, for the first time, of delicious backward glances. Kavanagh would concentrate only on the present: 'Write about that pint on the table in front of you', he would bark. He stayed at McDaid's, and the world came to him on a daily plate. The Kerrigans stayed at the Four Courts Hotel. We agreed to meet that night. We did, and bumped into the most magical umbrella holder for generations in Irish literature – Liam Miller of The Dolmen Press, a genial, rushing-about-town druid. He carried the proxies of a whole generation of writers. Manuscripts and proof copies in those days rained down at Miller's office and house on Baggot Street, or his printing works in Upper Mount Street. The world was a new lounge bar then, and we crossed over Baggot Street to Phil Ryan's upstairs. Miller, the Kerrigans, and I immediately were in the thick: the barman, Peter Tipperary, so loud and clear – serving the Ulster poet Bertie Rodgers, who, between barnaps, monologued about the archaeologist Estyn Evans. The Kerrigans blinked, smiled at Bertie's plus fours, took a drink, and were in the circle. At late closing time we danced through the trees in the middle of the road to Miller's office, to the whiskey bottle and a gleaming array of Eric Gill's books and bookplates in the case. For Tony, it was his first night as Panamanian-Irish in the heartland. It was not as great a fable as the one Tony liked best to talk about – the eight hours of Picasso talking and drawing while Cela looked on like a cat – but enough to swing and shine on. I imagined Oscar Wilde whispered to me, 'Life is the nights after the opening night'.

Prancing time. A long, long, perhaps sappy spring. Kerrigan had the wine-king mind. The American academics promenaded up Baggot Street: Max Rosenthal in bow tie; John Unterecker, quiet voiced, eating in the cafe above the Brown Jacket book shop. In the morning, on the same stretch of street, one would meet Kavanagh advancing from Parsons Bookshop towards Harry Street: 'What news, foreign or domestic?' he would greet. Frank O'Connor's wife and pram would come down the pavement. Kavanagh would wait patiently in the doorway until they had passed.

Friendship was a village no one ever left without a drink in hand, a melody of lights and brights. Tony and Elaine, their son Camilo Jose – Cela was his compadre – and their daughter Antonia had moved into the top floor of a tall house in Fitzwilliam Square, to which was added, a week later, a white Mercedes down below on the street. Were there enough coins on the mantelpiece to put petrol into it?

We all thought the Baggot Street summer would be endlessly renewed. John Berryman slid down the banister of the morning stairs of the Majestic Hotel as Liam Miller and I called. At the foot of the stairs he hopped into the bar – all without a word. A bottle of gin was put in front of him, and it would be a few minutes before he'd talk. Our poetries got up, circled around us on the bar floors. Mine was that of the bog flower ephebe – 'boy' was interchangeable with 'girl'. Tony Kerrigan's was unabashedly male:

> The clatter bones are puky bones
> compared to Mary Jordan's bones
> which shimmer in her milky hands
> like milkmaid's making – morning hands.

And still I live in hopes to see
the Holy Ground once more.

Kerrigan would get down on his knees and forget the Bollingen Foundation, for which he worked, whenever he saw any of the innumerable Mary Jordans. He would worship her hands or any parts of her body that made music, her fingers on silver spoons bearing oranges or leafing figs: 'Fine Girl You Are!'

My sister met Paddy Kavanagh. As his poems show, he liked women medical students. He took her several times to the Shelbourne Hotel and paid. He invited her to go to America with him. When various personages – Billy Wicklow, James Pope-Hennessy – moved between tea things, Kavanagh would say, 'A woman has nothing to fear from that man'.

Kerrigan's cavalier in attendance was Liam Miller, allowing Kerrigan to tilt in the whirlwind, making him a non-abstract reveller, and Miller the Playboy of the Eastern World. When wives were far away, in cars or cabs we screeched on bad tires through the backlanes of the Irish Sea; we had with us, say, a girl whose uncles had drunk five farms in Tipperary. She lay on the taxi floor when we passed the prying uxorious window. Miller and I were content with porter on non-whiskey nights; Tony wanted oysters and porter:

Mary Jordan's fountain hands
fingers gushing water
Georgian spigots on her knee
tapping fountain water.

Kavanagh was in The Bailey. He looked out the window and saw a notable Dublin figure escorted by Miller and Kerrigan. He commented, 'Christ crucified between two thieves'. He never threw a word to Kerrigan, but there was reconciliation with The Dolmen Press. I joined the publisher and poet for a photographing session on Baggot Street Bridge. These later appeared in *Self-Portrait*. As we went down to the canal bank, architectural students on the roof of the almost completed Bord Fáilte building cheered. Kavanagh gave his GAA referee's smile.

On Leeson Street, on the corner with St. Stephen's Green, over a grocery, and opposite a student pub, Tony's exalted master, Edward Dahlberg, waited for us: another cave occupied by Aladdin and Plato, shone. He had two handmaidens in there, his Irish woman Julia and New York woman Renée. As Elaine, Tony, and I went up the wretched stairs we heard the great boom, 'I'm as lusty a Jew as Saul of Tarsus'. Dahlberg was the first person I had met who wrote exactly as he pounded the universe. There he was in a nineteenth-century dream, wearing some kind of nightshirt with stocking cap, in armchair. We were ministered to with glasses of wine; Julie and Renée withdrew. Edward thundered at length about Gareth Browne and other 'senoritos' of the 'Beerage'; Tony and Elaine pondered his talk of friendship with a young man and its golden alleyways. The two 'mujeres' walked about the house. In the room, the hallway, the kitchen were five thousand books just unpacked – soon to be crated again for Palma or New York's Lower East Side. As I progressed at intervals to the bathroom I found the women having their own colloquium on the edge of the bath. Was Renée talking about Henry James? I found out it was her doctoral dissertation. 'You naughty girls, having your own drinking party', I said, and thought – a better 'milagro' than what was happening in the sitting room.

In the Kerrigan apartment at Fitzwilliam Square there seemed a lot of space with very white walls; you would expect the Mediterranean sparkle outside the windows. Elaine brought in a mantilla-black tray with dazzling, sizzling tapas. How I loved rinones a la Jerez. Julia's head was bent down. On the couch Tony and Dahlberg jerkily conversed, the two Bollingen Foundation buddies, the silversmith and the goldsmith. All is not well; conspiracy surges: Tony has been taking too many pills and vinos and they are trying to persuade him to go to Dean Swift's House of Rest, St. Patrick's Hospital. They tried the day before but by the time the cavalcade of two cars got by the entrance gate, admissions was closed. Tony seems unplugged from the scene.

Meanwhile Elaine focuses on another problem: how to keep Dahlberg out of it. I am providential as I escort Julia and the towering over-coated figure down the stairs. Dahlberg's white hair and grey mustache preside over brooding in the Pembroke Bar. Sipping and sighing over glasses of stout, we lament the world's end, the Falls of Troy and America. The expatriate, the protégé of D.H. Lawrence, the friend of Hart Crane in waiter-fights in the Dôme, shifts to his familiar ground: Charles Olson, the Neptune of the New England waves, whom Dahlberg wants to dispatch:

> Olson's mother was an Irish biddy. When I used to stay in their house she would always give him the bigger meat cuts. Right in front of us she would put less on my plate ... *Call Me Ishmael* is all my book. Where is the dedication to me? ... It's on page 51.

Tony Kerrigan wrote a postcard to me from St. Pat's – did they have them for sale in the front office? – saying yellow is the colour of madness. I belonged to another religious persuasion and was saying prayers under the stained glass of McDaid's. McDaid's was a religious experience – a right number of priests, a set of vestments. Towards evening, benediction, and especially inspiring were the voices of the Latin choir. Besides Paddy, John Jordan was often the celebrant: 'Blessed be God, in His angels and in His saints'. To whom, exactly, were we referring? I can only say we were not awash in Rilke's angel-ghosts. The day's prayers had been long; the crowd was often tired. From noon to about eight Paddy Kavanagh would be coadjutor. I often noticed him slipping out at lunch time for a chop in a local eatery – he was not amused that this was observed. The language of the premises was Irish-native rural. On some days it was, 'It's five pounds to talk to me today':

> 'Paddy, it's usually only a pound, even on a bad day'.
>
> 'But it's a black day for me – give it to me or fuck off'.

I held up a one pound note. Paddy took and savagely, if calmly, tore it to little pieces. Some gent got down on his knees, in that small lounge behind the single pillar, and scooped the green remnants up. It now hangs, framed and suitably inscribed, on a suburban wall.

Bacchic discourse, contrasted with the apparent 'reasonableness' of Miller and Kerrigan, occurred in other dissension centres. Paddy drank Scotch and consumed vast quantities of baking soda. In Mooney's of Baggot Street he quoted Dr. Johnson on friendship: 'A man should stretch his legs under the table'. But I was always running off to see friends. Once, when he was staying in a nearby hospital but on parole in Mooney's, I showed him a photograph of Thomas Kinsella in *Time* magazine. It was not the way to treat a sick man. To make up for it, I took a brown paper parcel of Guinness to his hospital ward. He was sitting at a table in front of the fire. He took out a bottle and drank it; he told me that his hospital records were so interesting, the doctors were sending them to Harvard.

The list of places for frenzy is quite long. Once, on Merrion Row, we ran into Liam Miller and Katherine Graham, proprietor of the *Washington Post* and *Newsweek*. A fracas between Kavanagh and Graham broke out in the back bar of O'Donoghue's. Of course, a gent may not repeat certain words. Miller went away, bowed by the loss of opportunities for Irish writers in the United States. In O'Neill's of Merrion Row, Kavanagh said to me, 'You're bent but you're not as bent as Jordan'. Paddy came to the Gorey Fleadh Ceoil in 1962, and refused to take a drink from Thomas Kinsella in French's. Tom Kinsella, in the front section of the bar, offered a drink to Leland Bardwell, Gareth Browne, everyone in the group. Kavanagh growled, 'I wouldn't take a drink from you'. When Kinsella bought the round, Kavanagh remarked, 'He wouldn't buy a drink for me'. Paddy demanded that I take him out to my house in Coolgreany; my mother wouldn't allow it. He wrote up the situation in the *Farmers' Journal* – 'turned away like a dog'. After disappearing for the night, I found him and drove him back as far as the Dargle Tavern in Bray. Even to this day I can remember the spots where we had to stop along the way for nature's operations.

Then Kerrigan made his excursion to Gorey, which was about to follow Wexford, the county seat, and create its own extraordinary festival. Paul Funge, an original because the Faust type is unusual in Ireland, was beginning to assemble ideas and painters, writers, scene-shifters, choruses, and revellers. The place thickened, and a local teacher, Diarmuid Ó Súilleabháin directed the traffic and critiqued the growing swell. Kerrigan saw Ó Súilleabháin as the soul and medicine man of the culture, and stepped up his formidable courtship powers. The attraction was that Ó Súilleabháin was a Gaelic prose writer and poet, who had a number of books and awards. Alastair Reid had impressed on Tony how an article, a book, an account of modern Gaelic would be attractive; the *New Yorker* would be interested ... Then Kerrigan found Ó Súilleabháin to be a tango dancer like himself, except this was with republican politics, greyhounds, racing. So, he fell upon him and he was co-opted. Liam Miller was brought in, the wizard of print who made words on the page possible, when Dublin believed nothing was more beautiful.

A book was born in three languages: the original Spanish text of Borges, who had composed a map of Ireland that is not imaginary, for nothing is other than possible here; Englished by Kerrigan; Irished by Ó Súilleabháin; and bound in bright colours by The Dolmen Press. It flew from the cuckoo's nest of Buenos Aires, to us. Nothing illustrates better why I preferred Kavanagh's bohemia to the other one. When Kavanagh visited my home town, he came as himself, with no idea of work in sight; he was there, he rested, he wanted to go back. Borges could have imagined Kerrigan and Miller, but not the man from Mucker. I joined the aristocracy of all day in the pub, ultimately justifying the comment of May O'Flaherty of Parsons bookshop: 'James Liddy is a nice man, but he has never done a day's work in his life'.

A favourite abode of Kavanagh's was Leland Bardwell's basement flat at 33 Lower Leeson Street. As the party progressed after closing time, Paddy slept on a couch in the corner. He would not show any sign of life, except for the hand that went in under the pillow and released the noggin of Scotch. He drank in his sleep. Once I was there with a friend and Kavanagh woke up and was in tears. There was no one in the basement; before closing time, everyone had gone to the pub. He kept saying he was dying, would we send out for a *sagart*? We were close to the Jesuit house on Leeson Street; we considered knocking on the door, but the crisis was averted. People started coming back from their rounds; parcels were opened: life is all the days after the opening day.

I drove Paddy home many times: to two different houses in Leeson Street, to Upper Mount Street, to the South Circular Road, and other dormitories. I drove him for the last time to the Amiens Street Railway Station in August, 1967 – just before I hit the San Francisco trail. He told me in the car that everything had gone 'except the liver'. Paddy Kavanagh was as heterosexual as Baudelaire or, I might add, Miller or Kerrigan. The night he died, as in Paris on another occasion, there was discussion among his intimates as to whether he died a virgin. I doubt that, because he loved life like a farmer's son, and because of his friendship with Katherine. One of his favourite phrases was 'very entertaining'. I liked him because the man was not ruined by the gift of great poetry. I also liked him because he was derisive.

I lose sight of Kerrigan and find him only in 1990, just before his death. He's in Notre Dame, Indiana, just a state and a bit away from me, going by Lake Michigan. Our Vergil is Frank Corcoran, Irish musician and professor, who meets him in South Bend and brings us together for the last letter:

> I saw you at Liam Miller's in Mountrath. Willy-nilly, your image has slipped into my daydreaming all through the years since ... I've often told the story of my laying of the wreath of your *Esau, My Kingdom for a Drink* on the then un-imaged tomb of the other James, in Zurich, as you asked me to do (and as I reported in Terence de Vere White's *Irish Times*). Two nights ago I gave a talk on Cela. I'll send pre-publication MSS. (on Cela) from my Kellogg office when I return to North Siberia, USA. On *The Family of Pascal Duarte* I'm earning big bucks (50% of royalties to me: best contract ever, so please order your orderly students to order, per carita ...)
>
> You once told me that your M.D. had told you to walk before breakfast. His advice cost me nothing. So I took it. And this P.S. is penned on return from the dawn (medio dia) paseo, to buy USA's best and most teriversatel news-mongering paper, the *New York Times* ...

You have to take your choice among the bohemians. There were other coteries besides these two – for instance, the taxi squad around Brendan Behan, which careened to a stop outside McDaid's on many a late afternoon. This was a lively group which I could not enter because of my allegiances. Spent are the pints of everything. With Arts Council bursaries and the Aosdána run-around-the-ideological-mill, the Irish post-bohemia has lost, as Austin Clarke might observe, 'our intemperate habits'. The young on circuit or in Bewley's – you can lead them to water and they drink, but is it Perrier?

My era in Dublin's Grafton Street labyrinths, which bought its rounds with generosity and naiveté, seemed to gather for the last time when Paddy Kavanagh's widow, Katherine, died. The funeral, twenty-two years after the poet's death, brought the tribe of McDaid's together. Ever since Kavanagh's death, it had assembled on St. Patrick's Day, near his canal bank seat. Now it was time to say goodbye. We who had gathered around the flame were now dispersed.

In the Church of the Three Patrons, Rathgar, the coffin was still in the side chapel while the monsignor was robed on the altar. Three wispy altar boys rolled it along hitting legs, benches. Peter Fallon in the pulpit read the poem about Islington which Katherine told him was her favourite. The monsignor told how life was a divine poem streaked with light and darkness, it was like Caravaggio painting the way the subjects are seen. One journey was over and its reward was beginning. Before the coffin moved down the aisle a woman's voice sang 'Raglan Road'.

Outside, Miss King of the bookshop bussed everyone. John Montague did business with an editor across the way. Helen Moloney, Katherine's sister, went around asking if everyone had a lift. A turn-around in Carrickmacross to get to the Dundalk Road. Several welcomes to Inniskeen, a picture of the poet, a sign for Shancoduff, the birthplace, the cemetery wall, a tall lad with an earring, 'Where can I leave this wreath?'

The arts advisor to the taoiseach, Anthony Cronin, conscripts poets to carry the coffin. Pass by the stepping stones on the poet's grave, past his sister Annie's – 'Hope to see you all in paradise'. The priest wears a hunting cap to the delight of an American student. Over the words of the resurrection, Helen Moloney's echo.

'No, no, I can't let this funeral go on, Katherine has stated her wish to be buried beside Paddy, it is in her will'.

Mary, the poet's sister, says, 'Helen is right, she should lie with her own'.

The solicitor goes down to the car for the will. The priest decides there will be a delay of three hours while another grave is dug; the chairman of the Kavanagh Society gets up on a tombstone to reiterate the announcement. The mourners parade back to the social club, the bar is open, pots of tea and sandwiches in the inside room. The solicitor says, 'The Atlantical wires are buzzing'. Ronnie Walsh says, 'Kavanagh would have loved it'. The poet's great nephew, John Lynch, drinks Lucozade and asks for a fag. Soon he is drinking black pints. His great grandparents lie inside the cemetery gates and no one bothers with them. 'I'm glad I'm a Lynch, all the Kavanaghs are mad'.

It's time. The crowd throngs out of the hall, up the road, up the side steps, back to the place where its stepping stones have been removed. The hole is open. Mary looks into its openness, 'This is Patrick's grave'. She blesses herself with a piece of earth she takes from it. The last clays of summer are falling on Inniskeen. The poet is now old. The poets step forward to read a poem over Katherine's coffin down in the grave, Anthony Cronin reads 'Bluebells'. Michael Kane reads a local poem about the watery hills. Leland Bardwell reads a poem of Pearse Hutchinson written to Katherine. James Liddy reads, 'Surely my god is feminine, for Heaven / is the generous impulse ...' A local bard reads a poem in which butterflies stray.

– from *Eire-Ireland* (1995)

A Memoir of Parnassus

Who would Patrick Kavanagh dine with at journey's end? Obviously with Landor and with Donne too, if permitted English company. If the poet from Monaghan is confined to the Irish Heavenly Mansion then his feast guests must be James Joyce and Moore (Thomas). There would be Grace and quasi-animated remarks on theology; before glasses were once too often refilled, the discussion would move to the Union of Hearts with England. Each of them would be impervious to the loss of one or even four green fields – no one ever wanted to go to Belfast, they would agree, no matter what flag is flying over the bloody place. As talk gave way to a party: Joyce would turn mellow, barely restraining himself from dancing; Moore, red-cheeked, would itch to compose another lyric about the harp; and Kavanagh, just a trifle tidley, would contribute smuggling stories that took place across the Monaghan-Armagh border. Soon they would be trotting out song after ballad, yielding to the most mystical experience of their lives: the voice in Irish melody. A nest of singing birds, a Heavenly Mansion in itself!

Going home they would tell stories of their favourite British aristocrat, the wealthiest man who ever understood and liked their verses and rhythms. For Moore, Lord Byron would fairy-glitter again; for Joyce, he would be in Maxime's with Lord Carlow; and Kavanagh would tell his tale of an evening in Brooks' with Harold Macmillan and his son, Maurice. Each had a great search for the sophisticated person on the other side; each wanted to vindicate his race before a strange altar. For who but a poet would be able to witness to the aesthetic ideal of a quaking union of hearts across the Irish Sea, and who but Patrick Kavanagh could with integrity praise someone like AE for his stand against Wolfe Tonery ... For great poets are singing birds of peace and oppose implacably macho horror. They were doves of light heart.

In Ireland, if one is not a poet what is one? A gombeen man or woman, a lawyer, an accountant, a party appendage. There is also the horrible possibility that such a person is also a poetry lover! For that – as I saw in my youth with Patrick Kavanagh in the pubs off Grafton Street – you may be cursed and forever separated from any nest of singing birds. Moore would have done it with a turn of the small portly back; Joyce would have expelled with icy politeness; and Kavanagh would have (and did) interdict with a back of his hand accompanied with choice words. Their work was not a simple matter of 'making song' but their lives had that noise – woe to any that dared into the sacred fenced-off area of their private lives – though each for part of the day lived in public. Living in public was 'presence' sonorously consistent with the objective lyricism of their creative compositions. They had the literary virtues. They looked with an equally hard eye at the pattern of their experience and at the depth-charge of their sincerities which remains – technique. Kavanagh would keep reminding me of Pound's, 'technique is sincerity'. 'Beauty is so common a thing', Pound would have sung if he had been born Irish, 'so many drink at its fountain'. Irish poetry is not the repetition of Metaphysics, Metalanguage or Semiology that other poetries may possess – for Celtic poets are singing birds, not singing philosophers. Their violence is always directed at critics whether old soft-analysis or recent structuralist language-blandness. ('Talk about language, *mon cher,* but don't write anything in it'). Ultimately their bitterness may be directed against the reader who is not the poet, not the lighthearted silver-Tara-ed one.

'Go and deconstruct yourself', Kavanagh would have sung if he had been French (born in Brittany) at the Professeur.

Writing is only a postscript to hearing voices or, if you belong to one of the abstract countries like France or North America, voice. It does work against the completion of language because the artist's task is always abandoned or Valery-ed: 'Language itself can never language express'.

But poets confer poise and authority, their language, on words, not because they fret or worry about language – they accept its loss forever, going on the muse-dictation, inner cloud voice or outer planet sound, to make their statement, not ultimately reducible to teleology dismissal or to the manipulated ideology of the Signifier. The poet's script is insignificance, to which is added something not to be calculated in criticism or in system 'incorporation'. Perhaps, as in Kavanagh, poetry always effaces living, by breaking it to moment or page-moment.

Kavanagh knew in any case that living vanishes: 'Go and love without the help of anything on earth'. His text, like that of Moore, Joyce and others, had to be performed in the phosphorescent psyche of the Irish bog – thin Faustian mist for nourishment. Texts not visited by the evil Paddy spirit; they were aware, 'You can take the man out of Ireland: you can take Ireland out of the man'. Kavanagh was his own man, moon-detachable. Of the three writers I have mentioned, Kavanagh stayed the most in Ireland. What store did he mind more than they? Domestic pain. When I used to meet him on the street his greeting was often in the form of *The Times,* 'Any news foreign or domestic?' His life could be called the scripture of the ungrateful task. The story of a man who, unlike Yeats, had no magic: therefore you believe him.

Kavanagh, like every other major talent, selected what a writer does. He periscoped himself, rising out of the waters like Venus – Anna Livia. The exteriority of the media-world fascinated him; the BBC were zoological freaks – one had to ride and get cheques sometimes – but they were the cause of culture, folk or individual-visionary (Academe doesn't count at the crossroads), decapitating itself. His voice, his gravel of accent, was too dominant for smoothness of image. He was surrounded – who isn't? – by men and women of visible means and no spiritual supports; or you could say he was left almost alone in the ballroom of life with companions who had no dance steps in their minds as he had. On the wrong side of the North of Ireland Border, he also was born too soon for the Ulster poetry bash. Kavanagh never lived in a suburb where the monsters, Media and Reputation, video themselves. He didn't, like some of his younger colleagues, go out at night and when no one was looking (not even the stars) clandestinely put Blake's grain of eternity into the concrete block at the corner of the house.

He would tell me, 'Write of what's in front of you – that bottle of stout on the table there. That's it'. He didn't mean by this that you should write a poem on the price of the first pint you ever consumed – which is almost the eternal subject of radio talk-shows in Ireland. There were physical objects and, after them, morality, a code of style or an ethic of the Christian soul. Unaccustomed faces would, from time to time, appear in McDaid's of Harry Street – it could be Roethke or Berryman, or Spender, Guinness-booking. A night I remember is when Thomas Kinsella, Richard Murphy, George MacBeth appeared. Kavanagh approached Kinsella, 'It was a very friendly thing (review of *Kitty Stobling*) in *The Irish Times*. Thank you. Very friendly'. Kinsella, the ablest Irish poet since Kavanagh, replied, 'It was just my honest opinion of the book'. Kavanagh's attitude is revealing: he kept an eighteenth century code of manners which goes something like this: Of course there is merit but unfortunately only posterity will make the judgments so we won't be around to cash their cheques; but in addition to merit there exists (and strongly) personal communications and affinities. These as Sam Johnson (one of the most used Kavanagh sources) noted, must be 'cultivated'.

To be cold in the poem becomes cancer in literature. It is a form of spirit devilry, to try to hold on to the poem for one's own silent, wanton ways. Naturally it is your own clothes you must hang out on the Muse wash line. Clothes-line garments are never very pretty but they can be seductive: Public Relations, which prints contemporary writing as it prints everything, doesn't like the display. Kavanagh taught us young ones to stand up to them.

An interesting illustration of this is his reaction to 'Two Offerings for W.B. Yeats' which was published in my magazine *Arena* in 1965. He was living then with Richard Riordain and Robert McBryde in Upper Leeson Street. He looked at Tony Cronin's piece on Yeats in Cronin's usual journalistic-poetic stance:

> One prefers to be able to like not only the work but the man in most or many of his aspects. One also likes to be able to like the relationship between what the work is about, what it praises, celebrates or derides, and what we know of the man ...

and he looked at mine ('Yeats was the rare example of a "phoney" who made good because he was an original "phoney" and translated artificiality into sincerity ...'). He said, 'Cronin writes the usual rubbish. You have a real point of view'. He saw it as simply as that, as birds flying to roost with the twig from the Tree of Life in their beaks.

Though he was cut off from large areas of society because of his attitude, I believe Kavanagh was possessed of the afflatus of happiness. When I knew him, his health had given way, and he had perhaps used alcohol too much as a form of day-long liturgy, yet he had content in his work and was content with his life. His domicile moved more frequently than his pub but he was well rested in the sign-paths of his mind. I take him to have been a Christian; he had the secret quality of real traditional religion; he was tormented by the lies and lack of imagination of large sections of the human race. He hated bohemian parties and orgies: hence, the living at the pub which is at times the monastery where the writer could practice the necessary cruelty of solitude upon himself. He was a preacher of the comic spirit which is the human personality at play. He probably did not read the fragments 'On Pushkin and Scriabin'[1] which projects the real basis for a Christian view of art as always based on the idea of redemption ... Art is for art's sake and not as a social duty nor a hallucination, nor the market-place, nor 'structural possibilities'. Mandelstam sees clearly the keystone:

> Art cannot be a sacrifice, for a sacrifice has already been made; cannot be redemption, for the world already has been redeemed. What then is left? A joyful commerce with the Divine, like a game played by the Father with his children, a hide-and-seek of the spirit.

Not here the test and horror of the Father, not the assassination of the Father and his metaphors and images – but a game, always a new play, with the offerings of the Father, the Beginner, and a rehabilitation of language, exhausted by the thirty years rebellion of the professors stealing the clothes of Artaud and Mallarmé. Mandelstam comes closest to Kavanagh in the feeling of release into freedom with this Heaven-nursery aesthetic. The two poets draw nearest, maybe, in their related belief in personality. You have, they sang, despite the many, one soul and one life. Kavanagh presumed he was making poems 'through the flavour of personality'. His personality was powerfully exotic and that is part of the heliotropic effect of the poems, the bending under strange brain-light. The attractive tone of the latter poetry right up to the last poems vanishes towards the reader but the imprint and extension of it on the reader's consciousness is not erased. It is transformed to the next poem, monologue interior or exterior, and back again, just like that bottle of Guinness.

In the early sixties, Kavanagh was invited to a literary conference on 'Poetry Since Yeats', held at Northwestern University. He told me in Parson's bookshop before he went – in the tones of Padráig Pearse – 'The Fools, the Fools, they have already paid me!' He vowed to break it up after half-an-hour. He stayed true and vital to his promise; the result is available in the fourth issue of *Tri-Quarterly*. Kavanagh was defending his bride – Life; he was seeking the same risible word-at-play spirit as his own. He would not rest with the fools in the cool valley of Establishment. His confreres played the game, what became later on the bone-dry Derrida puzzle-game of the world – 'The worldness of the world' – Kinsella grimly (he knew the score), Spender oafishly with that 'curious English stupidity' that Kavanagh referred to in the symposium: Snodgrass owlishly and childishly – because Kavanagh found a free spirit like himself:

> In fact I would say the only people in America that are alive are men like Jack Kerouac ... the disagreement is simply between life and death and that is the key to it all. I believe in youth, in gaiety and fun. I'm not interested in boredom.

That was Kavanagh at play, after redemption, after the escape from meaningless philosophic and academic language, after exit to self-acceptance and the cultivation of the poetry-garden of middle-age. The identical words I heard him say, while I was a student and before I went to play in the taverns, at a meeting of the UCD English Literature Society – the meeting at which he also defended the Archbishop of Dublin's ban on playing football with the Yugoslav team (1956), and said of Yeats: 'Whatever you think of the bastard ... when he was around you always knew there was a poet in town'.

To get back to the Evanston symposium: an interesting aspect is the comments of the professor who organized the event, Donald Torchiana, who remarked in summing up on 'the usual stale Kavanagh clichés'. I can attest that his cliché is my truth; my life was changed by the evangelization of Patrick Kavanagh in McDaid's and elsewhere, even on very bad coughing and sweating days. The soul goes marching on!

I saw you on your wedding day but I didn't on your days of dying. I was in San Francisco and read the short paragraphs of the obituary in *The San Francisco Chronicle*. I wept and wrote an elegy which was, I suppose, the easy thing to do. You were, I thought, pure civilization, pure Irish Hellas. Solitude made in desert of pub. Father of us all. Ego-mother of us too, that joined us in the beginning to everything. Long-necked look of Orpheus, fatal glance. Wounded because Parnell and Redmond couldn't marry Ireland and England, yet Orphic eye that shouldn't have turned around on Ireland and did. Internal, emigrant, forsaker of exile. New Irish writer: the Kerouac of the North Circular Road, the Spicer of Baggot Street Bridge. And many other dreamers in the grass, many familiars ...

I ask myself this question: what would have happened to me if I had not met you in the morning of my life? I would have stayed lawyer and hung myself writing prose. But words alone are certain god.

– from Peter Kavanagh ed.
Patrick Kavanagh: Man and Poet (1986)

NOTE

1 Osip Mandelstam: *Selected Essays*. Translated by Sidney Monas (University of Texas 1977), pp 123–127.

In Memoriam: John Jordan

John Jordan was the most gorgeous literary man I ever set eyes and ears on.

He acted as the personal representative of the nineties in Dublin, a junior representative because around the corner from the pub dwelt Micheál MacLiammóir in his unlit house or dark silver-lined bower. John was the grandson of Oscar Wilde.

John chaired other languages. He flicked cigarette ash like Jean Cocteau. He steamed of love, sometimes like Verlaine, sometimes like Rimbaud; hot pub talk. High real love must be reinvented, John intoned. Maybe love can only be invented – at a party or in a bar at that. Across a smoky room let us invent you.

He came first in two short takes. On Dawson Street with Kate O'Brien and Lorna Reynolds, all looking like artificial national monuments. Later John told me, You know, Kate is not religious.

During a tutorial he asked each nun, in the front row, to construe in turn Marvell's, 'Had we but world enough, and time, this coyness, Lady, were no crime'. Sister, please inform us what is occurring here, what does the gentleman propose to the lady? One by one the young nuns rose and left the classroom, to gather outside like a flock of geese.

We settled down.

My orator. We went to the Edwardian restaurant, The Dolphin; marble, deep carpet, a drunken Earl on the broad stairs. In the dining room at lunchtime the day was very young, the waiters as drunk as us. I got into trouble, by waxing about my powers, give me a theme and I can write a poem in half an hour. John had no mercy, I suggested tipsy cake. We stormed delicately into its sherry. John said, when he visited Edward Longford in the afternoon, Longford would clap his hands and a footman stepped in with a silver tray of cream buns.

This must have been about the time John turned thespian.

Yes, John said, Elizabeth Bowen was right about Dublin of that period. Her trams gave her away, they crawled around with a rasping vibration, they gave off a dusty and charnel smell.

We were in a morning light, before the darkening behind a mask of words. The peppermint bloomed.

Dublin became a pub, a pub with side-excursions.

Paddy Kavanagh, the poet, was the pub. Other writers went in and out, but Paddy sat across the place, a multiple effigy. He said, Fee-Fi-Fo-Fum, Dublin is dead Dublin is dead, it's a black day for me. His clique were Yeats' blind beggars who have shelved responsibility. They spent their days rummaging up acquaintances to buy drink. John shone among them, as he wore a bow tie. We joined the party, it turned into the fifties. A Noah's ark: John the prophet, hallucinating among the doves.

John phoned the Vatican, the White House, by taking the pub phone off the hook, mouthing into it.

– from *The Irish Review* (1989)

A Memoir of Katherine Barry Moloney Kavanagh

To the memory of Patrick and Katherine Kavanagh:

> I was not important as I deplaned
> at an unimportant airport.

I knew Paddy before I knew Katherine, the man before the woman, that must have been the Irish order then. Paddy was fond of referring to Listowel as the 'Athens of the North', but he himself incorporated the famous daimon from the agora, akimbo and dangling he was the architect's sketch of the poet; tall as a contemporary glasshouse and as strong as a horse. An incessant clamour against things as they are and people as they must be, a diatribe in a pub encased in gravel and buttressed by scotch. That market place of whiskeys and porters shook with his beautiful pieces of savagery.

There were many occasions and teachers. John Broderick came into McDaid's armed with white shirts from Switzer's. Standing at the end of the bar he entreated, 'Queue here for free shirts'. Paddy jumped and came back with three. Sean Dunne of the Labour Party roared, 'Get that nancyboy out of this'. I learned advantage or adventure.

Paddy held satiric court in McDaid's with no wounds unexplored. To a woman professor from the Carolinas, who had to buy him three brandies before he uttered, he remarked he liked 'Eich'. 'You like Ike', she said. 'I mean Eichmann'. 'Are you that eejit', he asked the Archbishop of

Canterbury in Parson's. Archbishop Fisher's sin was he had attacked on the BBC the wasteful expense of the space flight to the moon. Profanations yet there was the angeled Mass-goer side by side with the daimon; Paddy leaning at McDaid's door praising the heaven come to earth he had seen at the Vatican Council's opening or avowing his friendship with Archbishop McQuaid in the context of the prohibition of attendance at the Yugoslav football march. Paddy was poet of the moment following the lunar, either the dark side or the light.

Paddy's commerce with women was mysterious; there were attempted liaisons with medical students promising them trips to New York and Tiffany's (my sister was one of them). He had courted seriously in his tea-room years before the drink; he had the country passion for the urban milkmaid.

A favourite abode of Kavanagh's was Leland Bardwell's basement flat at 33 Lower Leeson Street. As the party progressed after closing time, Paddy slept on a couch in the corner. He would not show any sign of life, except for the hand that went in under the pillow and released the noggin of Scotch. He drank in his sleep. Once I was there with a friend and Kavanagh woke up and was in tears. There was no one in the basement; before closing time, everyone had gone to the pub. He kept saying he was dying, would we send out for a *sagart*? We were close to the Jesuit house on Leeson Street; we considered knocking on the door, but the crisis was averted. People started coming back from their rounds; parcels were opened: life is all the days after the opening day.

There were still women around, mostly other men's women; for as Tony Cronin observed of the male court in the pub, 'Paddy who used not like them is now surrounded by them'. It was true: his court had expanded and gelled. Paddy's impression was only favourable in his crowd; Dublin expected but has never liked the poet as a ragged clerk, it much prefers the radical. Also the city could never wear a country boy as clever as this. It was my consistent duty on Friday afternoons to drive him down to Amiens Street station, for the weekend in Inniskeen with the sisters who would first of all put his feet into a basin of hot water. He was taken care of, how he needed that, drinking so much as he galleyed into old age.

But Paddy also went to London and stayed longer and longer periods there – inevitably there stole across the Irish Sea the rumour of a woman. This became more and more confirmed. Finally the poet was revealed as being in love, was Romeo and Adonis in the flesh, and was really looked after and was made happier. Soon Katherine, whom some knew already, would be coming over.

Katherine was in McDaid's coming over to me to give a little lecture on how to treat Paddy. She was apparently uncomfortable with Paddy's new-new friends from UCD who had gypsy-gathered for this talk there ... Gins rapidly in hand, she shone as the empress of the small bar and tiny lounge. Confirmed, she joined in every discussion and began to laugh. She was the sports and racing friend of most, especially of Paddy O'Brien, the head barman of Leinster. But Katherine really was the patria, in the core of its dreams, tastes, evasions, and secret glories – history sparkling in her eyes, uncle Kevin the 18 year old medical student hanged by the British, and her father James 37 days on hunger strike during the civil war.

Shortly afterwards in London I went into the Museum bar and heard Katherine's voice in the distance. I didn't think I was quite her friend yet and hesitated. I realised she was Gloriana with a London packed around her huge as Buckingham Palace. I didn't go and kiss hands; the only Katherine I ever knelt to was Dublin's and Grafton Street's.

She had come home. There was intense buzzing and planning; I was not admitted to these secret councils. Dr Riordan and others convened about; finally my best and most affectionate medical pal Tony Carroll told me it was the ultimate: the bans. In two days time at the church where James Joyce's mother had met his father; I had to hurry my wedding suit but Tony and I were there.

The ceremony was in progress at a side chapel. Twenty or so Bohemian folk watched as the nuptials were shuffled through despite odd outbursts from the husband-to-be. These cries of seeming dissent were probably only factitious comedy and I hesitate to record them. At the 'Do you take' stage, I may have heard 'It has nothing to do with me'. But what else does a man say? I heard afterwards that the great friend, the Archbishop, had instructed the officiating priest to ignore all side rumbles. Done, and when asked to go to the sacristy to sign the register, the poet tossed his mane, 'Bring the fucking thing out here'. Done, and soon the party was streaming across Rathgar Road. The *Evening Herald*, that evening, ran the photograph with the caption, 'Bride and Bridegroom leaving church'. It showed Dr Riordan, keys in hand, and Paddy Kavanagh walking towards the car.

We proceeded up to the bride's house off Rathgar Road for the first reception. We were introduced to the mother lying a-bed, an older version of Mise Eire! Tony Carroll's neck of the country woods appealed more to her than mine, though her sister Madame O'Rahilly told me she had known my father well in college. The bridegroom wandered uncertainly about the room until he was presented to Mac O'Rahilly. He began to discuss Mac's father's death in 1916; Paddy said, 'That must have been a terrible end, dying drop of blood by drop of blood and no one could come to him for the snipers' cross-fire'. The O'Rahilly paled. Right over to Eoin and Joan Ryan's house, once owned by Joe Hone, the biographer of Yeats. Paddy couldn't eat the nuptial foods and an omelette was prepared for him. We sat on the floor of the spacious drawing room around Paddy who sang for us his favourites including 'Lord Ullan's Daughter' and 'Raglan Road'.

I met Katherine and Paddy one morning and went to their flat off Palmerston Road: how exhausted and down Paddy was while Katherine was cheerful. Next week my sister met Paddy who chased her around the cake stand at Bewley's, gabbing about Katherine. I drove Paddy home many times: to two different houses in Leeson Street, to Upper Mount Street, to the South Circular Road, and other dormitories. I drove him for the last time to the Amiens Street Railway Station in August 1967 – in stalled traffic in Pearse Street he told me every organ was gone 'except the liver'. This was said with the same brio he had once used in Baggot Street hospital when I saluted him with half-a-dozen Guinness. 'They're sending the records to Harvard'. He listed for me among our friends and writers who was malicious, who was innocent.

Paddy Kavanagh was as heterosexual as Baudelaire or, I might add, Miller or Kerrigan. The night he died, as in Paris on another occasion, there was discussion among his intimates as to whether he died a virgin. I doubt that, because he loved life like a farmer's son, and because of his friendship with Katherine. One of his favourite phrases was 'very entertaining'. I liked him because the man was not ruined by the gift of great poetry. I also liked him because he was derisive.

I was cabled in San Francisco, 'Paddy Kavanagh Died Yesterday'. Sure enough it was in the morning's *Chronicle*; I went to Market Street for the *New York Times* and found the obituary sub-heading. 'Reputation for Eccentricity Said to Have Overshadowed Talents as a Writer'.

In the summer Katherine was living in a basement flat on Fitzwilliam Street, surrounded by friends. Martin Green and others came from London, her sister Julie back from San Francisco. 'The Hill' was much in prominence. Katherine started working for her family out in

Chapelizod. Her life was packed; she had our madness for sociability. She liked to go driving on Sundays which was too reminiscent of my father for me. She travelled to my two places. Coolgreany and Kilkee for my birthday parties: in the former there was dancing in O'Rafferty's yard, the latter contained an afternoon of pints under the ceiling-wellingtons in Mrs Chambers' premises – Katherine denounced the Welsh people with Atlantical pride. By now she was living in the basement of her father's house (we had to make no noise going upstairs to piss). It was not good for her to have to prepare the parental tea at an exact time.

Julie died, crashing off the freeway to San Francisco airport on the way to collecting *The United Irishman*. On Katherine's bed lay the tricolour from Julie's funeral; we were often in that room drinking until the wee hours; it was a museum gleaming with Kavanagh memorabilia. One night Katherine presented me with the last shirt Paddy had ever worn, it was red; she also gave me some signed editions. I said, 'At least Paddy's shirt is a different colour from Yeats's'.

We went on an expedition to London – Eddie Maguire and others to a Con Howard 'do' at the embassy in honour of Paddy. I spoke alongside that mildly offensive man, John Hewitt. Afterwards in a famous Irish pub, Katherine washed away my chagrin with her comedy and sympathy, 'I know you didn't like it, pet'. Katherine then decided to pay her first (and only) visit to the States. She had relatives in New York but she was also coming to see me in Granville, Ohio, where I was teaching. She arrived with Carlos, a young American about Dublin town. Jim and I entertained them royally in The College Town House until the madness was in our glasses; in one of my nasty 'fits' I threw Carlos out because he made a speech praising the United States for what it had done for his family. Poor Carlos had to sleep the night in the car. Katherine soon linked up with some hippies in my classes: she went out to stay at the farmhouse rented by Link Freeman and his friends.

Then in Newport with Hank Schlau we had the time of our lives; that was what Thames Street was for sailors. An absolute passion for expression tore up the sidewalk; Jim's Place had a fight every five minutes: we felt Hart Crane stalking around – we stayed in a hotel over wind and water with few guests; three beds in the room, Katherine in one and me in Hank's bed with no result; lamentation and joy of drunkenness. Once we came back with a black cabman; Katherine postponed the fare-paying by throwing her arms around him and saying she was with his struggle. (She did the same later in Times Square, at a newsstand; she liked Brezhnev and the people's movement everywhere). We took a bus from Newport to New York that passed through Harlem and went to stay at the Chelsea Hotel; we liked the cooker and the fridge in the room, so unlike home. Some time was spent in intricate negotiations with Katherine's brother-in-law, Peter, whom we met for dinner in the Don Quixote next door. What Peter in his autobiography takes as a highly thought-out plot, by Katherine and me, to deceive him about Paddy's estate, was for me just a continuation of our alcoholiers, just another luminous lost evening; in the middle of dinner Peter went back to his apartment and presented each of us with signed copies of one of his major Kavanagh Hand Press publications.

James Moloney died and Katherine never seemed to recover from this – or maybe this was a coincidence as she now had medical troubles of her own; whatever the cause, Katherine seemed to slowly sink into an agitated, less self-reliant, state. There were still excursions and occasions; journeys to friends in England and cards from there, 'Got card in Lavenham – tourist village of Suffolk. Off to annual visit to "The Dell" (Elizabeth Smart). Ring me 19th. Hope your mother is OK'. We went up to Inniskeen to see Paddy's grave; Katherine was not immensely pleased with Peter's poem-stepping-stones to it. When I was to go back to teaching, Katherine always came to Grogan's to say goodbye; these were the American wakes of the late 70s/80s; Paddy O'Brien contributed a naggin of Irish to my journey, nature's old fashioned gentleman. Katherine got more and more difficult to get out; the last time she came to Grogan's she complained of the cold and about her friends; Paddy O'Brien made a valiant attempt to get the usual sports conversation going with her. But Katherine was down, as down as Paddy had been, without the celestial spark.

One of the last times we went to dinner with her was to a Chinese place on Clarendon Street she liked; there was no one there. She told a good story: Mac O'Rahilly had died and she had gone to her uncle-in-law's funeral. The Bar, the Judiciary, were there, no politicians except Rory [Ruairí?] Brugha, a family friend. Katherine noticed some military men saluting; Garret the silken Taoiseach was paying respects. Nobody seemed to be talking to him – she went up. 'Thank you very much for coming'. The Taoiseach replied. 'The old Sinn Fein families should stick together'.

She would only go to lunch at the restaurant in the Rathmines town hall. I was in attendance several times: again it was fairly miserable but Katherine did her best; told a good story. She was canvassing for the Greens, they knocked on the door of the General Secretary of the Communist Party of Ireland; it was opened by Mrs O'Riordain, 'You are welcome, come in, your late husband's friend toured the USSR with Michael'. The wife of the General Secretary did the correct thing; she opened a bottle of real vodka. Around the corner Chaim Herzog, the President of Israel, was visiting his boyhood home. Over the cheers Mrs Riordain said, 'We have a candidate, new to the Party, in the area, he won't win. Michael and I will give you our number 2'.

Her house was reconstructed; Katherine now lived in the upper part, shorn of its period grandeur. She had arthritis and someone had to open her cans for her. Someone else had to open the bottles of Guinness; the special pride of a daughter of Erin maintained supplies. She was a little cranky now about her friends coming out to see her; she held soirees on Sundays, attendance was enforced. A round of phone calls preceded them. As I was in the country, I could pick a weekday. She turned back now into her civic, revolutionary roots and at a pretext would attack my Blueshirt ancestry; once when I was in the bathroom she kept knocking on the door crying 'Fascist, fascist'.

The last story she told me was this: It was the first day of Spring, the Feast of St Brigid. Ever since she became ill she went to the nearest church, though she didn't like the priests. It was the same Church of the Three Patrons where she had been married. Bells in the distance; it must be the 9:30 Mass. A man stood at the church doors; she asked him, 'Is the 9:30 about to start?' 'Oh, you're a bit late, the 9 has been going for a while'. She peeked inside to see if the spotlight was on – no beam was streaming on any of the Three Tall Statues on the wall above the altar. There was no light on St Brigid on her day, neither was there any on Patrick and Colmcille. She stumbled out, she saw a man she knew on the footpath, she shouted over, 'I'm never going back there again, I'm finished with those men'.

May she and Paddy be sharing the same cup tonight.

– from *London Magazine* (1999)

'Pity and Love Are Beyond Our Buoys': The 'Simple Tale' of Austin Clarke's Politics

'A Simple Tale' is a poem in *Flight to Africa*, published in 1963, at the middle phase in Austin Clarke's poetic late flowering. It concerns Pat Rourke, a labourer who foolishly, like some before him, becomes a reverse immigrant, returning to Ireland with 'wife and babes' to find a job. His name is obviously chosen for racial simplicity and stereotype, with its dropped 'O'. Rourke finds himself in an underworld of deprivation and death; he sleeps in a coal-hole and hears the squabbling Dublin gulls around the offal and the dogs and cats around the dustbin. The coal-hole grows into a hell-hole. The family is broken up when Rourke is brought to Court, presumably for cruelty to his children:

> The cost – three pounds a week for each:
> Both safely held beyond the reach
> Of mother, father. We destroy
> Families, bereave the unemployed.
> Pity and love are beyond our buoys.[1]

The returned-to place turns into a perversion of the beautiful and the useful. Clarke customarily transforms his voice in his later work into a mock persona of the modern Irish State – a *patria* that denies elementary rights to its citizens and threatens the natural association of the family, guaranteed by the Constitution. The 'We' of the poem merges in a profound consciousness of national guilt, apologizing for a country that seems leprously anti-humanist and lacking in dignity and decency. Compassion begins outside the state, at the point where the territorial waters cease (with a hint of an 'Our Boys' network).

Clarke's political and social vision is as strong as it is locally focused – indeed sometimes its indignant points become so loudly formulated that it passes over into that hysterical passion lauded by Yeats. Definitely rooted in an Irish tradition, both Gaelic and Anglo-Irish, it is yet surprising to see from time to time Clarke glancing over his shoulder at contemporary ideologies. The placing of 'mother' before 'father' in the third last line of 'A Simple Tale' strikes an Irish reader as unusual. There exist a number of poems with interest in and commitment toward the cause of women, notably in the 'Martha Blake' sequence and in the stunning roll call of patriotic names in 'The Subjection of Women': Maud Gonne, Eva Gore-Booth, Hanna Sheehy Skeffington, Dr. Kathleen Lynn, and above all Countess Markievicz:

> She knew what their poverty meant
> In dirty laneway, tenement,
> And fought for new conditions, welfare
> When all was cruel, all unfair.[2]

Feminism is bound into ideas of social reform through this poem. Work on this level, however excellent, might justify George Brandon Saul's remark on Clarke's latter opus 'as sociological grist mainly'.[3] But Clarke rarely makes a statement of his politics on an abstract or international level; the liberation and amelioration of the cabbage patch becomes a permanent moment in a world revolution whose dimensions he never is explicit about. His difference with other important poets of the left seems glaringly visible here: they speak for socialist consciousness and for all people with a buttressed ideology, whether titanly as Brecht for his period between the wars or Neruda lyrically for the southern part of his hemisphere. Clarke stays on the stony soil, limited in extent, of his Irish inheritance almost Marxless.

In this literature we have, for instance, to substitute the Irish Civil War for the Cold War or, at the very least, the Spanish Civil War. Clarke took from Yeats the burden of keeping the political and historical ikon of Ireland going in poetry. Later in time Clarke's tone is inevitably more skeptical and less inflated than Yeats's also sometimes dubious evocation of events. There is a wary eye thrown over 'The workings of the fanatic heart'. Clarke as a political commentator displays more consistency than Yeats, because of his socialist cast of mind. There is a rigidity in Clarke's personality and attitudes that made him less of a practical politician for his own work, and he possessed, in a diminished way, a sense of movement (as can be seen in the contrast between Yeats's poems on contemporary fellow writers and Clarke's). The comparative neglect of Clarke in Ireland today partly lies in the fact that Yeats is 'flashy' and has more technics in his vision, while Clarke has more to say on actualities. The university-educated but conservative mood of affluence can summon little interest in a writer whose body of work consists of reproaches to its motives.

A poem on the opposite page to 'A Simple Tale', and using a good deal of the same vocabulary and intention, is 'Street Game'. At a famous four corners of the Coombe the poet observes a group of Protestant children on an outing with their Bible teacher; at the intersections they are heckled by Catholic kids from the slum area. We have the replay of a mini-Belfast in Dublin, though Clarke is ambiguous about the date of this encounter (it is unlikely he imagined it):

> Suddenly Catholic joylets
> Darted from alleys, raggedy cherubs that dared them:
> 'Luk, feckin' bastards, swaddlers, feckin' bastards!'
> Too well they knew the words their mothers, fathers,
> Used. Silent, the foundlings marched along the street-path

With clink of boot-heel metal. We have cast
Them out. Devotion, come to the man-hole at last,
Bawls: 'Feckin' bastards, swaddlers' feckin' bastards![4]

The reader notes common phrases and ideas from the other poem: 'the man-hole' in the street with its idea of confinement and underworld whose 'Devotion' – code for pious bigoted Catholics – instigates the verbal confrontation. Again 'mother' before 'father' though this may be a little left-handed, reflecting on the 'sacramental' power of women in Catholic society. The literally impish irony in 'joylets' contrasts with the emotive word 'foundlings', a codeword for Protestant orphans often suspected to be Catholic illegitimates proselytised to live in what was known as 'a bird's nest'. The parents instill this language of sectarianism, swelling it in the poem to a chorus culminating in the 'We' we are familiar with. The rerun of collective assertions, such as this, reflects Clarke's dynamics.

'We have cast them out' is more definite in time and statement than the earlier 'We'. Susan Halpern notes this voice:

> In his latest work, as much if not more than ever, he is the poet *qua* Irishman: his poetry evokes what it means to be an Irishman with a sense of his history in the contemporary world.[5]

There remains no doubt this is the Yeatsian 'We' though I worry about Halpern's ultimate phrase. Clarke's psyche was reared too medievally to be at home in the present; hence part of his restless disagreement with it. Unequivocation is master here. The force referred to is Daniel O'Connell's nineteenth century Catholic peasant Nationalists who took power in the twenty-six counties of Ireland in 1922, on the Treaty settlement, and whose ruling style, while outwardly correct to other elements, remains intolerant and chauvinistic. After the creation of the Irish Free State large numbers of Southern Irish Protestants left the territory; in his poetry Clarke is anxious to defend and protect the minority status of their remnant. Clarke is a loner here, not born into the Reformation Community, in fact quite the opposite; a Dedalus remaining at home seeking to publically assert the right of dissent from the privileged neo-theocracy of the merged collaboration of church and state. The voice is that of the unmentionable: the lapsed apostate Catholic quite naked for all to see, without benefit of exile or 'lapwing'. Clarke's role must be paralleled in other post-colonial societies. Nationalism and puritanism with a racial cast frequently rush into the vacuum left by the retreating colonial power; the pressure to conform seethes especially at the beginning. Immensely precarious at anytime, the poet and intellectual – both at times perforce the critic of their 'native woodlands' – is in double jeopardy at this juncture of new Caesar and old Christ. No one should wonder at the stridency of Clarke's polemics in the unrewardable position of post-Independence literary rebel. The generation gap between Clarke and Yeats comes from the fact that the latter was father, strangely, to the new state while the former is its dismayed child. The child is father to the man again, in political wisdom.

The spectrum of Clarke's themes expand beyond the Catholic-Protestant lopsided adjustments. They encompass various areas and to get the pluralistic multiplicity of them it is necessary to classify the different groupings of poems. Some of those categories overlap but it seems to me that Clarke is best served by fixing attention on the related interests of his political muse. Here are some:

I: Poems about actual political events in Ireland

Here the surprising fact emerges that over the years Clarke was a continuous commentator, almost a poetry newsman, as Maurice Harmon has written, following bardic eulogy, satire, and elegy.[6] He begins with poems on the Civil War itself, advocating a precise Republican anti-treaty point of view as in the lines on the Free State Establishment.

They are the spit of virtue now,
Prating of law and honour,
But we remember how they shot
Rory O'Connor.[7]

This comes at the beginning of his career but the development of comment stays constant with pieces on the new statue of Wolfe Tone, the mock re-enactment of Emmett's trial in the same courthouse for tourists, The Common Market, and interestingly on the burial of the great cultural patriot Douglas Hyde. The latter was a Protestant though an ex-Head of State; the divide stretches between the Cathedral and the street outside:

Two Catholics, the French
Ambassador and I, knelt down.
The vergers waited. Outside
The hush of Dublintown,
Professors of cap and gown
Costello, his Cabinet,
In Government cars, hiding
Around the corner, ready
Tall hat in hand, dreading
Our Father in English.[8]

The irony is all the more savage, for an Irish reader, when it is realized that the poem was published on the eve of the Vatican Council authorizing the Mass, including the Lord's Prayer, to be said in English. Other examples abound: 'The Last Republicans' wraps up that tradition from the time of the Civil War to the IRA campaign of the fifties; 'A Young Member of the Party' is a vignette of Fianna Fail, the corrupt majority party; 'New Liberty Hall' shows the vanity and distortions of the Labour Party now that it is an entrenched bureaucracy; or 'Christmas Eve, Dublin 1959' the description of a riot of festive poor.

II: Poems of direct social protest

These would include his pieces on children burnt to death because of inadequate precautions in orphanages in 'Three Poems about Children'; the various satires about pilgrimages to Lourdes or Fatima (happily Clarke lived before the Pope's visit to Ireland and the rise of the national shrine at Knock); or the immortal poems including the long 'Hippophagi' about the commercial trade in horses. 'Cypress Grove' is one of the most sustained of Clarke's middle length poems about the spoiling of the environment; in this instance, the ribbon building around Dublin's gracious old estates and villages.

> The sewered city with a rump of suburbs
> Has reached the pillared gate in its expansion,
> Design of the daffodils, the urns, disturbed by
> Air-scrooging builders, men who buy and sell fast.
> One Gallagher bought the estate. Now concrete-mixers
> Vomit new villas ...[9]

The detail, the practical nature of his protest, his irate moral swan-song for a vanishing of beauty, read remarkably. There are few second-half twentieth-century poets dedicated to the virtues of citizenship as Clarke. He eschews the large issue for the real loss.

III: Poems of church satire

A good many of the more biting poems, with extra sting in their technically complex tail, belong to his life-long Voltairian obsession with Catholic church evils. He brings to this vein of bitter perception both amusement and an obsessive quality which make his gift look medieval. Favourite subjects here include both old and new elements in the church: Irish-American conservative cardinals such as Spellman and Cushing and some grotesque effects of Johnnine liberation. Towards the end of his long service to anti-clericalism there appears a hint of regret and even apologetic admiration for his old adversary. In 'Nova and

Vetera' he wheezes out a thunderous elegy for the modernist victims of Pius X's Gestapo-like purge in the early nineteen-hundreds, but he wonders 'when cruel centuries are done' will Von Hugel and George Tyrell be raised as the new saints. And in 'Catechism Lesson' he sees the Council and John XXIII almost ushering this in:

For, arrogant, as the ages
Of persecution, greeted,
Escorted by Ecumenical Councils,
Heresy walks the street.[10]

I once asked Clarke, at the height of his fervor, how long it would take, if this process of ecclesiastical 'warming up' proceeded, for him to rejoin the Church. He avowed it might be 'two hundred years at the very least'.

IV: Poems denouncing sexual repression

Robert F. Garratt has drawn attention to the 'comic-erotic strain' that increasingly demands to be heard in the later Clarke.[11] The doubling of energy places the poetry close to the intuitions of Patrick Kavanagh's vision; it establishes what may be Clarke's most effective liberation commitment to the moeurs of modern Ireland. Here occur many of Clarke's classical pieces – the tightness of marriage in Ireland, the ignorance and hatred of sex surrounding it, contributed powerful and chiselled lines. An example is the fine lyrical description of the trapped couple in 'The Envy of Poor Lovers' and the searing tragi-comedy of marrieds in a primitive rhythm method:

But shall the sweet promise of the sacrament
Gladden the heart, if mortals calculate
Their pleasures by the calendar? Night-school
Of love where all, who learn to cheat, grow pale
With guilty hope at every change of moon![12]

Clarke is a great poet of the negations; he roars at his best when defending what would elsewhere be seen as part of the good and affirmative. He slaughters the opposition, which he would implicitly recognize as clerico-fascist, in matters of love and sex, and their concomitant privacy, with a special eloquence. He ranges far for auxillaries in his task. In one poem he describes with brilliant wit the erotic manners of Rousseau; in another 'Anacreontic' he portraits Lady Caroline Lamb who, having danced the Sir Roger with Byron and Samuel Rogers, unpetals, 'as the moon rose', the rose-bud of the translator of Anacreon. Who is no less, of course, than Thomas Moore the begetter of Anglo-Irish Literature and the drawing room moralizer of the Victorian era.[13]

V: Poems of Irish Literature politics

Clarke was noticeably sardonic about his contemporaries and peers in the second phase of the Renaissance. Sometimes this attitude, partly based on jealousy and otherwise on temperament, is tinged with regretful affection as with A.E. and Stephens. But in 'The Plot' the writers are not quite jestingly condemned; in his stricture on 'our lot' I see a sense that he felt the work they produced, that became received, did not address the real problems of the land. His insecurity as an artist was almost certainly contributed to by Yeats's exclusionary attitude towards him. His tiger reaction to this, finally mellowed in old age by a soft semi-forgiveness, can be traced in 'Abbey Theatre Fire', (two poems) 'A Centenary Tribute', 'In the Saville Club', 'The Echo at Coole', and other places. But the wounds of Irish writers are never fully bound up. Yeats was always the friendly big tree blotting out the ground.

Perhaps there should be other categories of his polemical talent. A case can be made that his many early poems of loss of faith prelude the major derivations of the more than jingling sarcasm. Another grouping could be built around purely personal poems, like 'Usufruct' that narrates the condition of his mother's will that his fine house at Templeogue go to the Church after his death and not to his family or 'The Knock' a real or imagined visit of a Jesuit to his house to subtlely inquire after possible repentance (this seems very much the paranoid plot of the Irish lapsed Catholic, suspicious when told of any clerical intrusion). Again, in the 1967 volume *Old-fashioned Pilgrimage* elements of a dark vision of America as an imperial predator occur randomly in the poems dealing of a visit to the United States. This is not taken very far; his poem on Pablo Neruda is charming, playful, and ideologically neutral.

Questions proliferate about Clarke. What motivated this unique poetry? His fear of an Irish cultural disaster? Where lay the source of this anxiety? In an Americanized, or a narrowly Gaelic, takeover? Or an almost Orange distaste for Roman Rule? The latter must have been the most potent cause – it seems a little savage in the Irish sense then to acknowledge Padraic Fiacc as the sole heir of Clarke's fiery laurels. For Fiacc, the cleansing witness to horror of Belfast in poetry as daringly virtuoso as Clarke's, defends his people, the Catholic working class. He shores up their atavistic self-image. The contrast exhibits not only a different time but Clarke's main preoccupation: an omnibus defiance of authority. The creed is that of Dedalus issued with the same cry, 'I will not serve'. Clear non-allegiance, non-conformity to the tribe at the psychic level. Clarke's justification would have been that he would accept only a society not at variance with his own ideals. No luxury like this is permitted to Fiacc or the poets of succeeding generations. Clarke possesses the fortitude of Padraic Pearse: the conscious instinct that one is embarking on a struggle that is going to be lost, set in the mood of ebullient self-defeat.

The brio of Clarke in his partially self-imposed isolation has defeated critics who do not understand the joyful pleasures of hermit-like obscurity. Thomas Kinsella writes tellingly on one consequence to the average reader of Clarke when he says in the introduction to *Selected Poems*,

'It strikes no glamorous or tragic or rhetorical poses'.[14] One gets the impression often that Yeats was not Paudeen-free, at least not from the better educated sort. Kinsella refrains from referring directly to the politics of Clarke's content, though he makes up for this to some extent in the notes – such as his commentary on 'The Pill' and the reference to Martin Murphy.[15]

Clarke as a writer continues to make his readers curious, queasy, and uneasy; principally because there signal no tokens of acquiescence. Rather a not too lightly veiled state of revolt distinguishes the poetry. Clarke cultivated the condition of inner emigration, as opposed to the more fashionable mode of exile. He cherished the resistance, almost for its own sake. Yeats hoarded nothing of the same stubbornness. But for an epilogue we have to travel further afield, to Brecht. To rephrase a poem of his on Karl Kraus one might say, in conclusion:

> When the Irish Free State had been founded
> Only an obscure message arrived from the eloquent one.
> In a five hundred and fifty page book
> He raised his voice to complain
> That it was not adequate.

From *Concerning Poetry* (1981)

NOTES

1 Austin Clarke, *Collected Poems* (Dublin: Dolmen Press, 1974), p. 257.
2 *Collected Poems*, p. 434.
3 Ray B. Browne, William John Roscelli and Richard Loftus (eds), *The Celtic Cross* (West Lafayette, IN: Purdue University Press, 1984), p. 34.
4 *Collected Poems*, p. 256.
5 Susan Halpern, *Austin Clarke* (Dublin: Dolmen Press, 1974) p. 92.
6 *The Celtic Cross*, p. 48.
7 *Collected Poems*, p. 178.
8 *Collected Poems*, p. 250.
9 *Collected Poems*, p. 286.

10 *Collected Poems*, p. 380.

11 'Aware of My Ancestor: Austin Clarke and the Legacy of Swift', *Éire-Ireland*, XI, 2, p. 95.

12 *Collected Poems*, p. 196.

13 *Collected Poems*, p. 482.

14 Thomas Kinsella (ed.), Austin Clarke, *Selected Poems* (Dublin: Dolmen Press, 1976), p. ix.

15 Austin Clarke, *Selected Poems*, pp 202–203.

ULSTER POETS AND THE CATHOLIC MUSE

From where politics and literature overlap an Ulster literature has been produced in the last eight years since hostilities began, and it grows forthrightly more significant with each year of conflict. Poetry and what are called 'The Troubles' emerge and emerge again from intertribal action, a joint emotional chaos. There is a natural, if obsessive need, shared by most of the writers to describe the region's experience and to bring a perspective into the onslaught of political events. The writers have found this ground immensely disturbing and defeating.

The roots of the politics have a lot in common with the roots of the poetry, and the roots of the problem in Ulster have a lot in common with the state of Ireland. Though the Provisional IRA confronts the resident British Army, the conflict issues from the people. The violence in Northern Ireland is indigenous. The consequences give Ulster writing a self-accepting impetus. For this the social and political crisis had to occur. Seamus Deane makes the point that 'the odd fact about the Northern poets is that their appearance now seems both belated and inevitable, because a good deal of what they represent has had no previous experience in Irish Literature at all'.[1] The difference is that, this time, the embattled writing has a more regional flavour. I say 'more' advisedly because the Gaelic eighteenth-century poets of the Sliabh Luchra area had an equal sectionalism. The idea of inevitability flows from Irish history: each political convulsion has spilled over into letters. One needs but to trace the insurrectionist sentiments behind nineteenth-century writing. I cannot agree with Deane about the unique place of the Ulster poets. Their experience, with its involvement in death and civil destruction, seems archetypically Irish. There must be added to that a complexity that arises from the adjunction of guerrilla warfare to contemporary sensibility – a sort of final *déjà vu* that lacerates the least Swiftian nerve.

Irish literature and violence had its previous testing in the Rising of 1916. Led by poets, its principal idea was a union of Christianity, Gaelic myth and Irish history: 'The people itself will perhaps be its own Messiah, the people laboring, scourged, crowned with thorns, agonizing and dying, to rise again immortal and impassible'.[2] This nationalism in connected to ideals of race as well as common humanity, with implications of sacrifice and blood-letting. Conor Cruise O'Brien characterizes this ardor as 'suffused with romanticism, which in politics tends in the direction of fascism'.[3] For artists, dangerous fascism means support for an unjust state, and none of the poets born in Unionist families countenanced the Stormont regime. Nearly as dangerous as fascism is the encouragement of undemocratic militarism, and no Catholic explicitly avows the IRA. The three most impressive poets of the minority – Padraic Fiacc, John Montague, and Seamus Heaney – stand aside from the actual conflict, though not without degrees of interior agonizing. Fiacc's and Montague's fathers both saw service in the IRA during the Anglo-Irish War. With the imposition of partition, and the defeat of the Republicans in the Civil War in the South, they had to emigrate to New York, where Montague was born and Fiacc educated. An edge is found in their work that is obviously absent from Hewitt, Simmons, Mahon, and others of the Ulster majority: a sense of calamity through race. Closeness to catastrophe, which could be called genocidal, animates most Northern Irish of the minority. It is embedded in the writing of poets, and it lies, somewhat hidden from view, in the prose of a novelist like Brian Moore, whose *The Emperor of Ice Cream* (1965) sets it in a Belfast location, and whose later novel *The Revolution Script* (1971), about the Cross and Laporte kidnapping, implies an equation between French Catholics in Canada and Irish Catholics in Northern Ireland.

Conor Cruise O'Brien does not allege that fascist sympathies are held by Ulster writers; he speaks of those engaged in hostilities, perhaps to warn young writers. The insights of the poets of this area are defensive, historical flashes of memory. Except for an occasional flourish by Fiacc, they do not write songs, as Yeats might have done, for the Samurai instincts of the young IRA soldiers. But they picture them. Padraic Fiacc's lines are so palpable that you feel he stands there:

> Irish kids sneer and jeer
> At, salute with cat
> Calls the dead body
> Of the young British soldier
> Gave up his life to save
> The Irish woman and kids
> Caught in the Spring
> – field Road Barracks
> About to explode ...[4]

Montague captures the pitiful, yet pitiless youngsters of destiny in the laconic brushwork of 'Heroics':

> In an odour of wet hawthorn
> arm-swinging heroes march,
> eyes chill with yearning.
> They sport dark berets and
> shoulder rifles as forthrightly
> as spades. Spider webs
> lace their sparbled boots.

A burst of automatic fire
solves the historical problem.
They drop to one knee.[5]

While the reader focuses on the primitive mindlessness, he is disciplined by other facets of the poem: the devastating irony of the penultimate line and the dandy exoticism of 'sparbled'. The barbarization of civilization gives raw material to both poets. These writers possess the force of political self-consciousness. They can, however innocently, take advantage of a pattern of violence to lay the foundation of an aesthetic success: they remain observers not participants. They return to the benign emotions described by Patrick Kavanagh, 'But poets as soldiers brings me to the quite scholarly and respectable theme of violence in literature, the violence whose heart is tenderness, not the other kind'.[6]

The violence in Ulster has been cyclic since the creation of the one-party state in 1921. Its birth was accompanied by dark violence, remembered by Hewitt and McFadden, the poets of the majority, as children:

... neglected shadows from my boyhood years.
the Crossley tenders caged and roofed with wire,
the crouching Black and Tans, the Lewis gun,
the dead lad in the entry, one by one
the Catholic public-houses set on fire.[7]

and:

I am of Northern Ireland: born
Behind a mattressed window when
the crossfire between love and hate
jerked a corpse across our garden gate.[8]

The latter extract is from McFadden's poem 'I Won't Dance' where, with what has become in many cases an accustomed hindsight, he opens with the repressed imagery of a surface, guiltless childhood. Only a gap of three years separates the births of McFadden and Fiaac in the midst of the 'troubles' of 1921. McFadden's concern is genuine, but his context seems weaker, less sincere because he must be less secure in his feelings. Many of the Protestant poets read like this: middle-class children, worn memorialists, look out at rage and bloodshed they cannot understand or enter into. Louis MacNeice's phrase for his kind, 'Banned forever from the candles of the Irish poor', applies to the whole range of possible sympathies that a nationalist-born poet automatically inherits. Fiacc and Montague, and Heaney in a quieter way, have been handed down terrible heirlooms. Fiacc remembers that:

> Between the year of the slump and the sell-out, I
> The third child, am the first born alive …
>
> My father is a Free Stater 'Cavan Buck'.
> My mother is a Belfast factory worker. Both
>
> Carry guns, and the grandmother with a gun
> In her apron, making the military wipe
>
> Their boots before they rape the house.[9]

Montague keeps the same ancestry:

> … Although again
> and again, the dregs of disillusion
> churned in our Northern parents' guts
> to set their children's teeth on edge;
> my mother hobbling to the shed
> to burn the Free State uniforms
> her two brothers had thrown off
> (frugal, she saved the buttons) …[10]

There is another world, the acted on and the reactive, distinct from the Unionist passiveness noted in the childhoods of Hewitt, McFadden, MacNeice. Both quotations refer to domestic deprivations; both have 'Free State' references. The struggle in the Anglo-Irish war had been for the independence of the whole island and the fathers had joined the nascent army of the Irish nation. The boundary talks, the last stage of the six counties partition settlement, removed hope: the minority population was abandoned to the Unionist power.

In Fiacc's poem we see the poet more present in the conflict than is Yeats in 'Easter 1916', Fiacc seems the first of a European species to appear in Irish writing: he is the holocaust child of a war that never ends, but finally gets to be described on paper. His guilt arises because he is unable to fulfill his parents' role; he cannot carry a gun. The surface of the poem is broken up, dismembered, like a dream that, as the title of Fiacc's latest book implies, becomes a nightmare. His poems centered on cannibal-like Belfast use brutalized imagery, staccato rhythms, and hard street dialect. They jerk, grimace, end suddenly to convey that there is no way out of the pain. Fiacc's lyricism reads out a Rimbaudian enactment of Hell. Fiacc is not typically Anglo-Irish in his verse methods; like Montague, but more heavily, he organizes a free verse technique apparently influenced by William Carlos Williams and the American Black Mountain School. Metrics, or any given syntactical formula, are dispensed with, for pain and death do not need these. The tense usually has to be the present.

A lot of Fiacc's work consists in looking at the wounds to himself and his community, at the political assault on Northern Ireland. The wounds fester; Fiacc feels it from the inside. In 'Son of a Gun' he runs from a bull: blind violence turns back on itself, or maybe John Bull, the foreign symbol of an oppression, itself helpless. Fiacc sees a British-Protestant nexus, from his cage, in these terms.

> And sodium chlorate and nitrates
> In the suburban garage
> In the boot of the car
>
> And guns in the oven grill
> And guns in the spinster's shift
>
> And ammunition and more more
> Guns in the broken down rusted
> Merry-go-round in the scrap yard
>
> Almost as many hard-on
> Guns as there are union jacks.[11]

The chant of these piled-up short stanzas conveys the overwhelming cast of fate against the poet, who cannot hold a gun, and against his people who are outclassed in numbers and weaponry. The paranoid vision of such poems nearly declines into sheer political poetry, though never just into propaganda, were it not for the sentiments of compassion in Fiacc's books about sectarian torture, dead babies, and children. He can even see the enemy his parents would have fought clearly. He says something bland to make a young British soldier grin, but the soldier's 'glass eyes', protected by rifle and radio, look past him: 'I am an Irish man/ and he is afraid/ That I have come to kill him'.[12]

The poems, often brief, catch the moments of ruin. Occasionally Fiacc writes a longer piece to get a comprehensive grasp of what has happened. In 'Glass Grass' he walks through the Catholic areas in 'scorched-cloth smell and smell of burnt flesh' from a car bombing. He is to give a reading in Ballymurphy, when a priest asks him afterwards if he can put himself into the mind of a killer, he lies '... I can't, but I can. I'm polluted'.[13] 'The Black' is in him, the poison born of violence. The poem attacks all those who can take it less easily: 'fat-faced politicians' and his fellow poets.The memories of the killings make him different; he is a freak too; and Belfast is quiet, 'a beaten sexless dog', waiting for the next outrage.[14] What is compelling is Fiacc's candor. No one is spared as each part of the horror is displayed, the commentary on heaven and hell, in the community and inside the self, offers no relief.

The early poems of Fiacc are pleasantly low-keyed, and like translations from early Irish nature poetry. The bright, clear quality is present in his work under consideration but to different issue. Lyric absorption reaches for social absorption. Terence Brown usefully indicates that Fiacc's Gaelic vision of purity is 'tested against brutally explicit images of sectarian warfare and guerilla activity'.[15] Initiation simmers in Fiacc and, though gunless, the model he fits seems the 1916 poet-captain, Padraic Pearse. The landscape of young men caught up, dying in terrible actions, reflects Pearse's ideals and poetry.[16] The sensual theme of the tearing flesh of young men in war, and accompanying dreams of their peaceful flesh, connects Pearse and Fiacc to Whitman. It excites these writers to consider a comradeship partly compatible at least with militarism – a sort of troubadour Samurai mixed with a Spartan discipline. Fiacc's 'Unisex' outlines this complex of sentiments:

After the bombing the British soldier
Looks up into the barbwired Irish
Twilight. His unflinching open eyes
Deaden, yet unvoluntarily flood
With the colour of tea
Drenches his combat jacket sleeve
Now he is hugging
Now he is giving
his male love
To a screaming fellow being he does
Not know if it is a man or a woman.[17]

The young have surrounded Fiacc: he has encouraged the writers among them and published some of them in his anthology *The Wearing of the Black* (1974). A great tragedy in his life was the assassination of one of these young poets – Gerry McLaughlin – who is commemorated in a lovely elegy in *Night in the Bad Place*.[18]

The two remaining poets of superior quality among the Northern Ireland minority, Montague and Heaney, offer more of a contrast between themselves and Fiacc, than among themselves. They are more self-conscious artists, their roots are as much anthropological and mytho-historical as embedded in the present. Their languages serve as a medium, to be infinitely and minutely crafted, not focusing on a message. Their lines conform to half-lost, pattern memories of Gaelic lyricism, the collected poems of both would read as a reliquary of sometimes nostalgic impressions. They, with Thomas Kinsella in the South, have replaced Yeats as familiar mnemonic model in Irish poetry.

Montague, raised and educated in Tyrone, a swing Catholic-Protestant county, began as a Southern poet, a young man in Dublin's difficult literary circles of the 1950s. He made his debut in its magazines, and his early poems were published by the Dolmen Press in 1958.[19] A second and more ambitious collection, published in London in 1961, possesses more references to his Northern childhood with glimpses of neighbours and local occurrences.[20] Village and townland life is already being assorted into folk imagery that wears a Jungian aspect. In *Tides*, a mixture of lapidary styles and short-lined poetry exploring a moon landscape of love, Montgaue looks consciously north where two centuries of factionalism is again emerging, and plans a book that attempts to take in the Northern conflict in its parameters of consciousness: to regurgitate and display a committed writer's position. *The Rough Field* (1972) does effect such a result, but not decisively. The poems, written in the decade from 1961, are divided into eleven sections that form parallel chronicles to the story of Ulster, edging back to its roots in the plantation of the early seventeenth-century of the lands of the Gaelic princes. These ruminations appear, at least to this reader, mostly heavy and forced; particularly unconvincing as poetry is the 'Hymn to the New Omagh Road', where a confused medley of comment, quotations, and seemingly half-hearted 'real lines' obscures every facet of the passage except its intent. Montague's inbred use of marginalia bestows an archaic look. The problem with *The Rough Field* is that it suffers from two conscious flaws: myth-making and book-making. Too many of its poems are culled from previous collections and set into ill-fitting contexts. Examples are 'The Siege of Mullingar' first seen in *Arena* in 1964, and, less harmfully, 'Like Dolmens Round My Childhood, the Old People', published in *Poisoned Lands.* What remains brilliant about the book is the series of family vignettes and anecdotes told with a quiet intense particularity. Memories of a divided, and in many ways betrayed, family haunt Montague, his exorcisms raise the wonder of true art. His poems about his father, 'Stele for a Northern Republican', 'The Fault', 'The Cage', and in *A Slow Dance* (1975), 'At Last', present a Vergilian persona in Hades. Montague seeks in vain, but with great love, to reincarnate his father – the failure of reinvention puts his father into a distant limbo:

> ... But what if
> you have no country to set before Christ,
> only a broken province? No parades
> fierce medals, will mark Tyrone's rebirth,
> betrayed by both South and North;
> so lie still, difficult old man,
> you were right to choose a Brooklyn slum
> rather than a half-life in this
> by-passed and dying place.[21]

Terence Brown finds, I think rightly, a 'certain portentousness' in *The Rough Field,*[22] and suggests that Montague hedges on his Ulster commitment, or at least balances it a little dextrously with his avant-gardism.[23] This last accusation seems unfair in regard to the quality of the writing in his familial pieces. The steel of the political temper in Montague shines in an ideological poem like 'Penal Rock/Altamuskin', In *A Slow Dance,* in the poems that deal with the Northern tragedy, Montague has his eyes especially wide open: his reporting is both accurate and fixed in its finger pointing. In 'Falls Funeral', describing the burial of a murdered Catholic child, one senses a physical identification with the people:

A sight beyond tears
beyond pious belief
David's brethren
In the land of Goliath.[24]

His 'Northern Express', reminiscent of an earlier poem 'Bus Stop, Nevada', hits the center of the terrorism that sucks in most ordinary citizens:

A forced companionship of passengers tremble
by the sleepy roadside, attending sudden death.
Assistant shadow sprinkles petrol leisurely
over the back and sides of the Derry express
while chief shadow asks them to remove their boots,
the classic ritual before a mass execution.
Lucky this time, they are spared, warned off
to march behind the driver two miles in the snow
not daring, like Lot's wife, to look for the glow
of their former bus, warming the hedges:
their only casualty, thin socks soaked through.[25]

This poem has none of the modish trappings of parts of *The Rough Field*. Superb scene sketching, it grips the fear of Ulster: power is not drained away from the lines by ingenuous metaphor. There exist no panaceas, no ways to accept and sublimate what is happening. In this atmosphere the poet never offers any coy postures. He begins to make good on Hugh MacDiarmid's over-generous encouragement of *The Rough Field,* 'How far we are here from anything savouring of the Celtic Twilight'.[26]

In Seamus Heaney's three books before *North* (1975), a more substantial offering, *Death of a Naturalist* (1966), *Door into the Dark* (1969), and *Wintering Out* (1972), the strains of a younger poet are revealed. The problem is a rhetorical exuberance of language, which Heaney tries to temper with careful stanza-making in the British tradition. The landscapes, the pastoral episodes, are described but not felt in the way Patrick Kavanagh brings them alive in his Ulster country poems. We are reading a potentially good poet, a trial worker, one whose verse has attracted pilgrims. In *North*, the promise is partially fulfilled in half a dozen important compositions. Heaney's literary intelligence is being made to serve a quasi-mystical art in his well-accepted bog rituals. Heaney does not aim at capturing immediate life; it seems no accident Frost, and not Williams nor Pound, is Heaney's American connection. The poet celebrates the long dead buried in Danish bogs, human forms so fossilized that they form a museum-like background to the death that hovers over his home area and Belfast. In 'Baldberg' Heaney sets out the beginnings of his interest; in 'Bog Queen' Heaney uses first-person, short stanza narrative to describe the almost imaginary corpse, in grave clothes and cultural emblems:

> on the gravel bottom,
> my brain darkening,
> a jar of spawn
> fermenting underground
>
> dreams of Baltic anger.
> Bruised berries under my nails,
> the vital hoard reducing
> in the crock of the pelvis.[27]

In 'Grauballe Man', the account of the minimal decomposition has come almost to the point of nothingness: the poem asks 'who will say "corpse" to the "vivid cast", or "body" to the "opaque pose?"'[28] Heaney, who first saw the face in a photograph, keeps it as a memory-artifact and stylizes it by comparison to the *Dying Gaul*. 'Punishment' turns at the pivotal point of the book: the girl, weighed down with stones and rods and boughs and then dug up *inter alia* as oak-bone and black corn, is an adulteress, a sister to those tar-capped for going out with British soldiers. Heaney finishes the poem asserting that he understands 'the tribal, intimate revenge'.[29] Ulster violence cycles back directly to the primitive.

Heaney cleverly softens the harshness, even the cruelty, of his vision by building around it a pretty natural stage.

In 'Kinship' – a key word – the burial site is 'the love-nest in the bracken;' the scene is lavish with the softness of Irish bog and rain, 'seed-pod' and 'deep pollen bin' make a bridal bed.[30] The goddess comes out of 'the vowel of the earth' as the poem oozes out of the metaphored diction. The poet coyly admits he is a voyeur of death.[31] Increasing its sentimental impulses, this instinct phantasizes the coffins of dead relatives as those of murdered 'tribal' victims in a great funeral cortege driven south to the megalithic death chambers of the Boyne. The great chambers of Newgrange become a kind of funeral parlor where the beauty of the arrangements will act as arbitration of the feud.[32] Heaney has an unmeasured confidence in the power of his aesthetic neo-sadism to startle and impress his audience. One is momentarily shaken by the underground spirit of a writer willing to experiment with ever more extreme metamorphoses of the body. Terence Brown has commented on Heaney's passivity in face of the goddess. I, for my part, note his almost total inertia in front of experience. He is emotionally ambiguous, not quite certain how far he should dredge his researched feelings. This work has been understandingly summed up, 'His recent poetry has therefore seemed at times remarkably skilled, compelling poetic organization of his indecision, lacking emotional range and drama'.[33] Some critics have worried that Heaney has become the 'laureate of violence', in the words of one: 'a mythmaker, an anthropologist of ritual killing, an apologist for the "situation", in the last resort a mystifier'.[34] But the burden of attention, and given emotional birth and family pangs, some kind of identification, is inescapable. One must support the poet for facing up to it, even if one cannot always admire his planned rhetoric. A legacy from the animalistic violence of Ted Hughes' poetry must be allowed for. Bog is primal reality, and Northern Ireland seems to fall into it. Heaney exhibits a drawing together of history and landscape; the probing of Viking settlements suggests a later, permanent invasion. One wonders if the writer, in plundering the primitive resurrection, is psychologically exploring the roots of his own identity. The answer is not obvious.

Heaney is not restricted to burial phraseology in *North*. There is a section on contemporary events – a curtain raiser to which is a graceful and amusing lyric on Raleigh, Elizabeth, and the rape of seventeen-century Cork and Kerry. And 'Whatever You Say, Say Nothing' has sustained political commentary and a pleasant repudiation of Yeats' revolutionary attitudinizing. The poem should be sufficient to cower any critic who, conversely, imagines Heaney has not discussed the 'situation'. Two poems, 'Freedman' and 'A Constable Calls', are printed, with variants, in Fiacc's anthology as prose poems; here, the verse lines seems to squeeze out the tension. Still, they give us a satisfying view of the details of Ulster prejudice and paranoia. In the final poem, 'Exposure', Heaney appropriately confronts himself, secluded, an exile in County Wicklow in the South. He asks the real question, 'How did I end up like this?' But wondering about his friends and enemies is not sufficient, he must describe too much himself and lead into inflated mytho-history: 'I am neither internee nor informer; / an inner émigré, grown long-haired / and thoughtful; a wood-kerne / escaped from the massacre …'[35]

Fiacc, Montague, and Heaney deal only with the violence they cannot avoid; violence, to yield creation, must come to the writer in amounts he can deal with. Ultimately, we may have a great literature in Ulster, as we have had in twentieth-century Ireland. Perhaps the problems of the Ulster writer have already merged with that of the contemporary Irish writer. Stewart Parker, a Northern Irish dramatist, has recently spoken thus of the dilemma:

> I think any artist who stays in Ireland permanently is liable to be eaten alive. The artistic air that you breathe here is too thin to support you for a lifetime.[36]

It is by this precise thinness, this Yeatsian 'Great hatred, little room', this lack of peace and security, that the literature of the magical, deadly island has been nourished. As the greatest living Ulster and Irish writer, Francis Stuart, has remarked: literature is only to be experienced by those who 'dare pluck it direct from the tree of life'.[37]

– from *Éire-Ireland* (1978)

Notes

1 Seamus Deane. 'Irish Poetry and Irish Nationalism: A Survey', in *Two Decades of Irish Writing*. ed. Douglas Dunn (Cheadle, Chester, 1975), p.14
2 Padraic Pearse, *Political Writings and Speeches* (Dublin, 1924), p. 91.
3 Conor Cruise O'Brien. 'An Unhealthy Intersection', *The Irish Times*, 21 August 1975, p. 9.
4 Padraic Fiaac, *Night in the Bad Place* (Belfast, 1977), pp 15–16.
5 John Montague, *A Slow Dance* (Winston-Salem: North Carolina. 1975), p.38.
6 Patrick Kavanagh. *Collected Pruse* (London, 1967), p. 273.
7 *The Wearing of the Black*, ed. Padraic Fiacc (Belfast, 1974), p. 9.
8 *Ibid.*, p. 64.
9 *Night in a Bad Place*, p. 29.
10 John Montague, *The Rough Field* (Dublin, 1972), p. 39.
11 *Nights in the Bad Place*, p. 14.
12 *Ibid.*, p. 15.
13 *Ibid.*, p. 25.
14 *Ibid.*, p. 26.
15 Terence Brown, *Northern Voices: Poets from Ulster* (Dublin, 1975), p 144.
16 *Political Writings and Speeches* in general reflect this.
17 *Night in a Bad Place*, p. 19.
18 *Ibid.*, pp 47–48. Details of this murder were communicated to this writer in a letter of 30 May 1975.
19 John Montague, *Forms of Exile* (Dublin, 1958).
20 John Montague, *Poisoned Lands*, (London, 1961).
21 *The Rough Field*, p. 39.

22 *Northern Voices, Poets from Ulster*, p. 168.

23 *Ibid.*, p. 154.

24 *A Slow Dance*, p. 32.

25 *Ibid.*, p. 42.

26 Hugh MacDiarmid, 'John Montague's Ulster', *Agenda*, III, 2–3 (Spring-Summer, 1973, 112.

27 *North*, pp 32–33.

28 *Ibid.*, p. 36.

29 *Ibid.*, p. 38.

30 *Ibid.*, pp 40–41.

31 *Ibid.*, p. 38.

32 *Ibid.*, pp 15–18.

33 *Northern Voices: Poets from Ulster*, p. 183.

34 Ciarán Carson, 'Escaped from the Massacre?' *The Honest Ulsterman*, 50 (Winter, 1975), 183.

35 *North*, p. 73.

36 Stewart Parker, *The Irish Times*, August 13, 1977, p.12.

37 Francis Stuart. *Black List, Section H.* (Carbondale, Illinois, 1971) p. 105.

Ulster Poets and the Protestant Muse

An effect of a decade's cycle of violence in Ulster has been an undermining of Yeats's nationalist assumptions. A major poet partly because of pressures from the 1916 rising, the Anglo-Irish War, and the Civil War, Yeats devised in 'Nineteen Hundred and Nineteen' ambiguities, for example, that played between order and a vision of stark beauty in revolution. Southern Irish poets are now in turn becoming counter-analytic, editing and sometimes censoring this cultural tradition. A recognizable voice is in Paul Durcan's 'What is a Protestant, Daddy?':

> Protestants were Martians
> Light-years more weird
> Than zoological creatures;
> But soon they would all go away
> For as a species they were dying out,
> Soon there would be no more Protestants ...
> O Yea, O Lord,
> I was a proper little Irish Catholic boy
> Way back in the 1950's.[1]

The new confrontation with reality strips away Yeats's hidden antipathy for Irish Catholics – by 'Catholic' and 'Protestant' I mean one born into either faith – that can be found in many of his poems, such as 'Upon A House Shaken by the Land Agitation', and in his references to 'Paudeens'. This area of feeling was cloaked – and still is for many – by his heroic, personal forging of the idea of a nation through blood. It was also sustained by his art, but in the gross realism of the present decade his style has turned into matter for parody, as in Andrew Waterman's 'Derry Images, 1968–71': 'Romantic Ireland too lives on; / her crimsoned lips seduce; her tongue / knows no speech but bullet, bomb'.[2] As Yeats foresaw, the mocker is mocked; the old glory singer has become ridiculous. Patrick Kavanagh, the finest Irish poet since Yeats, sensed this move first: 'Irishness is a form of anti-art'.[3] The fact of sectarianism was kept from literature almost completely by all the Renaissance writers. The evasion was a legacy from the whistling in the dark of nineteenth-century nationalism. Is Belfast mentioned in Yeats? There is no reference to a writer living in Northern Ireland in Yeats's opus except Forrest Reid – and he cannot be said to have lived much anywhere on earth. What was AE's Armagh background? I am sure it was never discussed.

John Hewitt, born 1907 in Belfast, had to take notice of the streets, the atmosphere breaking around him. In his early work he alludes to discrepancy; in his later poems he makes in memory an evaluation of what he felt was missing, now regarded as wrong. It is not just the 'wisdom of old men' that makes him do this, it is Belfast on fire. The Northern state had not jelled as the Southern managed to do. Yeats had given the assent of validity to the Irish State late in life, in the late poems such as those on Casement and Parnell and with translation of O'Rahilly.

Hewitt withholds in 'The Dilemma':

> So, while my logic steered me well outside
> that ailing church which claims dominion
> over the questing spirit, I denied
> all credence to the stare by rebels won
> from a torn nation, rigged to guard their gain,
> though they assert their love of liberty,
> which craft has narrowed to a fear of Rome.[4]

The poem suggests the myth of corporate unity has not been achieved, only selfish aims. Paranoia and manipulation are not enough to hold a community together; romance does not exist in polarization. There was no equivalent of the pluralist attractions that Yeats could play with in Dublin. Wilson Foster in his *Forces and Themes in Ulster Fiction* remarks that Eden was the Reformation and conquest by the Planters of the rough Gaels, always imperiled by Catholics, 'fallen angels from their own Paradise'.[5] As Wilson Foster points out, the Protestant version is merely one of threatened loss, but the Catholic is the story of the Fall in which the Planters are the devil. The latter are obviously stronger, a binding myth, a reinforced atavism.

The artificiality of these divisions could not be long kept up in matters of the imagination. Even before the arrival of the disturbances in 1969 young Ulster writers were coming back to Dublin to reside and to enter Trinity College. Derek Mahon and Michael Longley are examples of this return migration. Seamus Heaney, Catholic in origin, came south in a different manner. Mahon and Longley seem longing but unable to quite fit in with Southern mores partly because of their poetic conservatism, a moral stance, and a feeling for metrical verse inherited from English practice and influenced by Philip Hobsbaum's group in Queen's University, Belfast. Terry Eagleton has observed the difference in Longley: 'His language is less gnarled and gnomic than that of most Irish nature poetry'.[6] Longley does not understand the Gaelic background; in his 'Letter to Derek Mahon' he alludes bewilderingly to the shadow of Patrick Pearse whose presence haunts the Irish-speaking parts of the West:

... We were tongue-tied
Companions of the island's dead
In the graveyard among the dunes,
Eavesdroppers on conversations
With a Jesus who spoke Irish –
We were strangers in that Parish
Black tea with bacon and cabbage
For our sacraments and pottage.[7]

Mahon, more sophisticated and mobile than Longley, has suffered transition better. But these two, by comparison to the other writers from the Protestant community, Hewitt and James Simmons, appear caught in the shock of displacement.

The ambivalence of Ulster lasted a long time. To writers of the minority, England was never their country, though a united Ireland could not be their residence. They knew the enemy in their own country: 'Ulster was British, but with rights on / The English lyric; all around us, though / We hadn't named it, the ministry of fear'.[8] Heaney sets out the ground to be recovered. Using the title of Graham Greene's novel makes vivid the Loyalist's hysterical World War II fever, while at the same time it suggests early the truth that Ulster writers of the minority – the poem is written to Seamus Deane, another Catholic poet – would receive initially not privileges, but negative responses. But the politico-military ambience of the partitioned province would elevate them to a unique opportunity; they would no longer be McFadden's poor versifiers – for the same opportunity would break for all poets of the region – 'born in an orphanage'.[9] Patrick Kavanagh had seen their predecessors with a cruel eye: 'As for the "Ulster" writers who comprise only the Six Counties writers, they seem to be insipid, colourless and with no particular regional flavour'.[10] Kavanagh is thinking of himself: he was born in Co. Monaghan, one of the three counties of the province of Ulster given to the Irish Free State by the Treaty of 1922.

The writer Kavanagh most names in connection with 'Ulstering' is Louis MacNeice, for MacNeice appears as the founding father of Ulster poetry, if a part-time one. He argued about whether he could belong to Ulster or could belong to Ireland. In 'Belfast', 'Carrickfergus', and sections of *Autumn Journal* he constructs a mnemonic model pattern tempered with an honest skepticism as in 'Time was Away':

> This land may seem a dreamland, an escape,
> But to her sons and even more her daughters
> A dream from which they yearn to wake; the liner
> Outhoots the owls of the past.[11]

He was in Ireland, in the South, when the war against Hitler was declared; he was swept with the natural jingoism of the Loyalist, however, when the reality of the conflict materialized. The blitz made him look at the native Irish state sourly:

> This neutral island facing the Atlantic
> The neutral island in the heart of man,
> Are bitterly soft reminders of the beginnings
> That ended before the end began.[12]

This reaching away – retching away would be a more fitting description for this piece – establishes a touchtone for Ulster writers that survives. They are different, specially the Planters' sons. The argument is complex because of MacNeice's fondness for his peasant, native ancestry. Yet with him, and other Protestant writers, the comity with the greater Ireland is not repressed. The attractions of gigantic sufferings in history, the wealth and splendid detail of the saga and lyric deposits in the Irish language, the leadership of revolutionary cause in the nineteenth century by brilliant graduates of Trinity College, provoked in them a penchant for reconciliation. MacNeice, in his postwar 'Western Landscape', returns to the need for roots in Ireland, not this time in Ulster but in the West, which he was perennially drawn towards. For all his founder's quality, he is torn apart between the real country of his youth, the environs of Belfast, and the Ireland of his romantic vision, the Yeatsian West, which he addresses in a proper filial mode: 'O Relevance of cloud and rock – / If such could be our permanence'.[13] Terence Brown in both his studies, *Louis MacNeice: The Skeptical Vision* and *Northern Voices: Poets from Ulster*, scrutinizes the divide in MacNeice and younger writers; and MacNeice was not totally of the heart, romantic in the native sense, charm substituting for excitement perhaps. Brown rightly comments:

> Yet it might be argued that the self irony of such verse, its skepticism in the face of romantic longing, its dogged realism, is that traditionally ascribed to the Ulsterman.[14]

I cannot go along when Brown suggests that Mahon takes up the note, and attitudes adopted, of MacNeice in his specific Northern poetry. Mahon's work is much smaller in scale, though pert. It is as if the younger poet's output were just MacNeice's Irish themes, a minor part of his *oeuvre*. But Mahon has the lachrymal response of the elder to their home town:

> But the hills are still the same
> Grey-blue hills above Belfast.
> Perhaps if I'd stayed behind
> And lived it bomb by bomb
> I might have grown up at last
> And learnt what is meant by home.[15]

One wonders how MacNeice would have reacted and composed if he had witnessed the tragedy of recent years – something strong and beautiful in its horror, following Yeats's Easter 1916 master poem, or a major telling of how it is?

John Hewitt takes up the watchdog position where MacNeice leaves it off. MacNeice's Drydenian, superbly rational style, baptized Hewitt's work and also the well-made verses of James Simmons. Heaney has noted the trademarks:

> ... for I'm talking of a certain literary style which arose from the "well made poem" cult in English writers in the late fifties and sixties ... In that sense, there is a kind of tightmouthedness which might be considered "Northern" by many in the South.[16]

Colin Falk, in a review of *A Man Lying on a Wall,* has noticed this element in Longley:

> There is a tight-lipped quality about Michael Longley's verse which could lead one to think of it as Protestant, not just in the sense that all art may have to be, but in a narrow and more restrictive sense as well.[17]

Most of these poets find it hard to give themselves generously. Over-trained, they hold back. We have a sense of poems processed at a too conscious level. In poems like 'Once Alien Here' Hewitt has candidly tried for some synthesis between Planter and native, semi-underground mythologies.[18] When domestic description, and the concept of 'nation' impaled on family and history, are tied together by Hewitt we get the good, searching poet who never raises his voice and obliquely sets the sequence of events, as in his 'Nineteen Sixteen, or The Terrible Beauty':

> Once, as a boy of nine, he heard his teacher
> back from his interrupted holiday,
> a red-faced, white-haired man, repeating wildly
> all he had seen of Dublin's rash affray:
>
> "The abandoned motor cars, the carcases
> of army horses littering the street ..."
> No more remains of all he must have told them
> of that remote, ambiguous defeat.
>
> It took those decades crammed with guns and ballades
> to sanctify the names which star that myth;
> and, to this day, the fierce infection pulses
> in the hot blood of half our ghetto-youth.
>
> Yet, sitting there, that long-remembered morning,
> he caught no hint he'd cast an ageing eye
> on angled rifles, parcels left in doorways,
> or unattended cars, he'd sidle by.[19]

The authority of poetry is working here as contrast with memory's fallibility. The latter quality is joined to the Loyalist child's myopia: a near-sightedness that signals how could it have come to this. The cosy feeling of 'remote, ambiguous defeat' goes forward to meet the reverberating of the exact 'sidle by'. The historical error finally appropriates the context: it was within a few years, not 'decades', that Pearse and his co-conspirators became sidereal through the fineness of their death and sacrifice. The title makes Yeats's nationalism stand out starkly. The great poet had half created the uprising; the embryo Unionist poet safely hides in the shallows. This feeling is aggravated by the blandness of largely unbroken iambic pentameter; in general Hewitt is pedestrian about prosody to the point of insensitivity.[20] Ulster poets do tend to get waylaid by craft considerations: they rest behind sterile walls of versification and would not amuse Ezra Pound.

There seems an aspect of Hewitt's poems that calls promptly for recognition. At least he is one of a very sparse number of Unionists who was aware of those outside his state and tradition. He wanted to raise the consciousness of his fellows. Bishop Daly outlines the problem in this fashion:

> The Ulster myth ... ignored the existence within its own State and territory of nearly half a million people, more than a third of its population, whose home had always been Ulster, but an Ulster totally differently understood, totally otherwise loved.[21]

Hewitt jauntily conveys this in ballad-parody:

> I'm Major This or Captain That
> MC and DSO
> This Orange lilly in my hat
> I sometimes wear for show,
>
> so long as I can walk my dogs
> around the old estate,
> and keep the Fenians in their bogs,
> and peasants at the gate.[22]

Heaney has been generous to Hewitt in his criticism, perhaps because of this movement towards his side of the racial division. It is not as easy a tribute as it looks: 'A stubborn determination to belong to the Irishry and yet tenaciously aware of a different origin and cast of mind'.[23] Hewitt has been at an unusual and solitary crossroads most of his life, but I cannot go along with Terence Brown who suggests that his career has been a failure.[24] Standing alone in a literary situation, conscious of an inner righteousness, does not imply an artistic defeat – quite the contrary. Hewitt has stood in the middle of the Ulster impasse, keeping his counsel, maintaining his connections to Planter and Gael. He is not disowned by extremist takeover; his patience seems all the more necessary. John Montague, who was born a Northern Catholic but has written as a Southern poet for most of his working life, possesses more lucidity than Brown:

> To be Irish was bad enough, but to insist on being Ulster as well seemed to drag literature to the level of a football match. But, as we shall see, Hewitt's instinct was right ...[25]

Hewitt's instinct was not a gamble, it was the discovery and retention of a subject matter that was embedded in every stratum of the social psyche. One cannot agree with Montague that Hewitt is 'that oddity in our literature, a poet of sustained political thought'.[26] He is rather a poet of political response, limited to one dimension. Though his sense of nationality has been thus fruitfully insecure all his life he has, in spite of it, become a spokesman for the moderates among the Unionist majority. The Irish leader, Jack Lynch, recognized this when speaking in commemoration of the 1916 heroes in the Garden of Remembrance, Dublin, in July 1971:

> Perhaps the national majority need to examine their consciences in relation to the national minority. Have our political concepts been sufficiently wide to include them? Have we been considerate enough about the things they

> believe in as passionately as we might believe otherwise? Do we agree that as John Hewitt writes, "they have rights drawn from the soil and sky" which are as good as any title held by any previous migration into Ireland?[27]

This is to remark that Hewitt is in fact an Irish nationalist, a more realistic one than Yeats.

The most considerable poet after Hewitt among the Ulster majority is James Simmons, born 1933, author of more books than any other poet in our period: *Energy to Burn* (1971), *No Land is Waste, Dr. Eliot* (1972), *The Long Summer Still to Come* (1973), *West Strand Visions* (1974) and *Judy Garland and the Cold War* (1976). These are all quite small collections, and their impact has been equaled by the influence Simmons had as the first editor of *The Honest Ulsterman*, not as apocalyptic a magazine as its subtitle once suggested. It is the work of a band of young writers who now wear the radical chic look of the late Sixties. Simmons has also stirred things up by singing his songs and ballads in public. Important differences between Simmons and Hewitt register themselves. Hewitt cares about the Northern climate of hate and violence and wishes to diffuse it by assimilating the two traditions. Until it hits him in the early Seventies, Simmons sloughs it off; but then he expresses his frustration and anger more in balladry than in direct lyrical pieces. One can see why the major Catholic poets – Fiacc, Montague, and Heaney – feel closer to Hewitt. Simmons does not necessarily want to become an Irish poet. He seeks detachment; he will not be the hanger-on or accomplice of Southern writers, though he writes of his hangovers like many down South. His work shows an attraction to the Anglo-Irish tradition that is balanced with a middle-class despair of the inclination towards political 'rumbles'. Holding off from the shambles of Belfast and Derry does not seem due to apathy, but in Simmons, Mahon, and other poets is an avoidance of the public theme to court the private myth – an elaboration, after all, of the Reformation freedom of leaving a man alone with his own conscience.

The individualistic vision of Simmons by implication impeaches the Catholic truths of sin and authority. It questions the clericalism of the minority, in particular it concentrates against a schooling that limits sexual enlightenment. His 'Protestant Courts Catholic' sets the two communities apart in a humorous, and possibly autobiographical, vein:

Intrigued, he argued, but she never budged.
She blamed the Church. He said she was a sham.
"You have to judge in order to be judged".
Her smile was roguish, false: "That's how I am".

"Look. I'm the serpent you have read about.
The law says no, I'd like if you would.
You're free either to stretch your fingers out
Or not. Choose, knowledge or servitude".[28]

Knowledge is Protestant, Miltonic free will and liberty; servitude a Catholic inferiority of the mind imposed by priestly restriction. But ideas are not violence and, confronted with the latter, Simmons can give as well as he gets, while loathing the exercise. The incident in the poem 'Experience' is filled with the tension of the Northern community. It reads like a gentle dip into savagery and complicity: 'A torn shirt and my lip numb and bloody, / my anger and – strange – the feel of my own body / New to me, as I struck, as he struck'.[29] Simmons's macho image, a skillful verse-mask, plays a linking part in the construction of his ballads that form his major statement on the sickness of his society. The three most prominent of them 'Claudy', 'The Ballad of Ranger Best', and 'The Ballad of Gerry Kelly, Newsagent' form a clustered outpouring of horror, in storytelling style, about three of the bloody incidents of these holocaust years. The first is about the Provisional IRA bombing a village without adequate warning, the second is a murder of young British Army man from Derry by the official IRA, and balancing these the third relates a killing of a Catholic shop-owner by

Loyalist thugs. There is an unequivocal assurance, in these words set to music, of the evil of such action. The writer's ear is well adjusted to the niceties of the poetic narrative, the perfection of tone clicks with the absolute morality:

> Sixty nine the nightmare started.
> Loyalist anger rose;
> sweet shops, butcher shops and pubs
> were burned down, forced to close.
>
> Who'd believe who never saw it
> the broken glass, the noise,
> voices shouting, "Fenian bastard".
> – little Ulster boys?[30]

This kind of forum for public questioning, which Simmons may have learnt from Yeats's late ballads, functions as a method of describing the inadequate motives behind an almost random and mindless round of horrors.

The intention to use craft stems in these non-Gaelic poets from the English tradition. They derive a tendency to write verse autobiography from the same source. The native poets – in particular Fiacc and Montague and, to some extent, Heaney – incline to the opposite: free verse experiment, fierceness of statement. Montague, in *The Rough Field,* follows the design of Irish poetics by publicly lacerating himself and family. Fiacc assumes even more self-destructive gestures in his dazzlingly obsessed *Nights in the Bad Place*. They almost blind the reader and obscure other dimensions in his work. Fiacc's search for a heroic possibility in life, in the midst of death, and for heroic figures to embody that possibility in art led to his editing of *The Wearing of the Black: An Anthology of Contemporary Ulster Poetry*. His Dionysian affirmation of joy, 'beyond all terror and pity – that joy which includes even joy in destroying', contrasts with Simmons and other Protestant writers. Simmons had attacked the anthology in *The Honest Ulsterman* alleging a bad odour surrounding the book from the journalistic 'nonsense' of its editor.[31]

Fiacc, in his reply, offers sarcastic nobility:

> The bad odour surrounding *The Wearing of the Black* is the bad odour of blood and it stinks of a society that has hopelessly degraded itself and consequently degraded those of us who have to exist in it. *The Wearing of the Black* is a mass of unpalatable truths that I have used and misused poetry to confront.[32]

And, admonishing Simmons, Fiacc says, 'Literature isn't created by good or respectable persons who never put a foot wrong'. It is true to say that among the Loyalist-born poets linger no traces of the Byronic hero, which was a dominant image in poetry up to the twentieth century, and whose recklessness infected the 1916 poets. Only occasionally is there risk-taking in their poems; it peeps out of Hewitt and parties out of Simmons. In any case, the city is burning.

– from *Éire-Ireland* (1979)

NOTES

1 Paul Durcan, *Teresa's Bar* (Dublin, 1976), p. 53.
2 Padraic Fiacc, ed., *The Wearing of the Black* (Belfast, 1974), p. 63.
3 Patrick Kavanagh, *November Haggard* (New York, 1971), p. 80.
4 *The Wearing of the Black*, p. 8.
5 John Wilson Foster, *Forces and Themes in Ulster Fiction* (Dublin, 1974), p. 9.
6 Terry Eagleton, 'New Poetry', *Stand*, 18, 5 (1977) 69–70.
7 Michael Longley, *An Exploded View* (London, 1973), pp 36–37.
8 Seamus Heaney, *North* (New York, 1976), p. 65.
9 The interesting remarks of McFadden on the earlier generation of Ulster writers in *Threshold*, 5, I (Spring-Summer, 1961), 25–34.
10 Patrick Kavanagh, 'Diary', *Envoy*, r, 2 (January, 1950), 85.
11 Terence Brown and Alec Reid, eds., *Time Was Away* (Dublin, 1974), p. 2.
12 Louis MacNeice, *Collected Poems 1925–1948* (London, 1949), p. 224.
13 *Ibid.*, p. 278.
14 Terence Brown, *Northern Voices: Poets from Ulster* (Dublin, 1975), p. 136.
15 Derek Mahon, *The Snow Party* (London, 1975), p. 2.

16 Seamus Deane, 'Interview with Seamus Heaney', *The Crane Bag,* I, 1 (Spring, 1977), 61.

17 Colin Falk, 'Catholicities', *The New Review,* 3, 28 (July, 1976), 56.

18 John Hewitt, *Collected Poems* (London, 1968), p. 22.

19 John Hewitt, *Time Enough* (Belfast, 1976), p. 18.

20 The problem with Hewitt's metrics is his monotony of form. His attitude is well conveyed in his unperceptive comments on Patrick Kavanagh's *Come Dance with Kitty Stobling* in *Threshold,* 5, 1 (Spring-Summer, 1961), 42–51.

21 Cahal Daly, *Violence in Ireland* (Dublin, 1973), p. 255.

22 James Simmons, ed., *Ten Irish Poets* (Chester Springs, Pa., 1974), p. 27.

23 Seamus Heaney, 'The Poetry of John Hewitt', *Threshold,* 5, 22 (Summer, 1969), p. 75.

24 Brown, *ibid.,* p. 92.

25 John Montague, 'Regionalism into Reconciliation: the Poetry of John Hewitt', *Poetry Ireland,* 3 (Spring, 1964), p. 113.

26 *Ibid.,* p. 118.

27 Conor Cruise O'Brien, *States of Ireland* (London, 1972), p. 265.

28 David Marcus, ed., *Irish Poets 1924–1974* (London, 1975), pp 86–87.

29 James Simmons, *Late Bat in Earnest* (London, 1967), p. 24.

30 James Simmons, *West Strand Visions* (Belfast, 1974), p. 40.

31 James Simmons, 'The Wearing of the Black', *The Honest Ulsterman,* 46–47 (November, I974-February, 1974), p. 68.

32 Padraic Fiacc, 'I Know the Faber Poets', *The Honest Ulsterman,* 50 (Winter, 1975), p. 134.

Nationalist and Worker in the Poetry of Thomas Kinsella and Thomas McCarthy

> artwork of our poor Republic.
> The prominent ruins that make Limerick Junction
> Seem like Dresden in 1945 ...
>
> – Thomas McCarthy, *Seven Winters in Paris*

'Artwork' in the sense of neglect or disaster was an endemic feature of most of the Republic of Ireland's visual history. Extensive British public building in Ireland in the latter half of the nineteenth century made sure a partially kempt State arrived in the 1920s. With triumphalist nationalism abating, and Limerick Junction still untouched, it is possible to note these ruins. Perhaps the new State had no chance of aesthetic function because of its beginnings in the Sinn Fein celebration of virtue that flowed as much, or more, from Maynooth than from the place de la Concorde. Yeats's last plays are implicitly concerned with the recent political and atavistic twitchings of morality; 'The Herne's Egg' has the concluding lines:

> All that trouble and nothing to show for it,
> Nothing but just another donkey.

I am sure he had this particular irredentist donkey in mind, among others. His next play seems to suggest it. If you burn down big houses you don't build railway stations. I recollect being in Limerick station, close to Limerick Junction, after arriving from Shannon, and a man coming up to me saying, 'There hasn't been a lick of paint put on this place since the British left'.

The lines of Thomas McCarthy, quoted at the head of this essay, and other train lines in his *Seven Winters in Paris,* take their edge from a prevalent poverty of pride, from a lack of sensibility about the appearance and shape of objects, and a willingness to put up with a lot or move quickly to destroy it. What region are we in but the kingdom of the dispossessed? A kingdom of mages, if you will, because we are not sure of what we have been dispossessed – something has been taken from us. Even if the trains run on time they arrive in the squalor of ruins. McCarthy's trains shuttle on different but adjoining tracks: they are emigrant trains with the suggestion of holocaust wagons; they often become exile coaches as in 'Gloucester Road Station':

> And all our Catholic distress.
> So lovely to escape the festering bog
> And the cowering Party hack!

Or wartime trains as in 'Buttevant Station' with its flourish towards Sean Ó Riordáin or even the Californian apparition engines of Eugene O'Neill in 'San Clemente Station'. The transportation of workers, labourers, soldiers, exiles, refugees, victims, mourners is a twentieth century perspective which equates transportation with displacement and murder.

Thomas Kinsella also carries poverty, and his lack of luxurious origin differentiates him to an extent from some Irish poets of the mid-century and later. Daniel O'Hara points out Kinsella's stance in writing is not fixed in the sublime or luminous but in the ordeals of understanding and suffering (66). Kinsella takes a turn towards Joyce and the quotidian. He does not abandon high modernism but offers it the direction of prose in poetry; what looks like Kinsella's obscure poetics is that part of modernism where prose can be bent to enhance poetry. Kinsella possesses a late great style, and it is an urban one like Joyce's. His trains go through cities and wastelands:

and we followed the rabbit tracks
dotted along light and powdery everywhere
and found the white silence
under a stillness of twigs
breathless with carefulness
where the rabbit went
where?

The season is Christmas, it is snowing and a bitter personal wound is explored that keeps an echo of Joyce's 'The Dead'. There is a relief from the knowledge of mortality, a de-sentimentalising of the past.

Kinsella's landscapes pace back to the Celtic presence, the hardly known but once possessed paradise and nightmare. The poetry undergoes atavistic memory,

by a salt-dark shore
by a standing stone on a dark plain,
by a ford running blood
and along this gloomy pass, with someone ahead
calling and waving on the crest, against a heaven
of dismantling cloud ...

The look back to *The Táin* is a journey to the founding ruins, to where perhaps the Dresdens commenced on this island, and from where if at all discoverable they might become a rite of elucidation. This poetry could be a catharsis deductible from history, a down payment on 'ordeal'.

Always at my back I hear Stephen Dedalus's chariot of fear. The train may be a modern chariot where Cuchulains and Medbhs go on board to their trysts in the fashion of Larkin's 'Whitsun Weddings'. McCarthy's poems of trains describe a rural diaspora in which hope mixes maybe with sexual love. It becomes impossible for me not to paraphrase Yeats: Man is in love / and loves what vanishes down the track ... Kinsella has paid his dues here, in 'Handsclasp at Euston':

> I bow to the cases cluttering the rack,
> Their handles black with sweat of exile.

Kinsella, the civil servant, is in that bow, as McCarthy so often in his poems performs the librarian. Their modes of walking terrains can also be contrasted. Kinsella's peregrinations are frequently, though not always, peopleless; he deviates from his exemplar Joyce in this regard. The obvious exceptions are his wife Eleanor, Sean Ó Riada, ancestors, and figures encountered in childhood. In one of his Republican Aeniads, Kinsella tours the battlefield as it reposes in the hill, streets, and river of Enniscorthy, Co. Wexford. McCarthy has more humdrum characters in his generally shorter poems; there is more people space on his pages. But I would like to emphasize that both poets are ideologues, taking their party pieces from the grittiness of history. McCarthy rambles around Paris in somewhat the same political fashion as Kinsella in Co. Wexford, although he is more forward in his identifications. Primarily, McCarthy snatches relics from the Third and Fourth French Republics but the Dublin and the Cork poets freeze their allegiances to the founding revolution of 1789.

Both writers are aware of possible nightmares concealed in the virtue-proclaiming Arcadia, particularly Kinsella. The question they have to deal with is: is there an affordable price to pay for a republic of nationalists, workers, and labourers, so conceived? Despite their commitments, these writers map the punishment inflicted by history on their Republic, ideal and actual. Their poems are in part the record of freedom scars. Their work varies from that of their predecessors in the Literary Renaissance in that the witnessing vision comes not from the shadows of the Celtic twilight but from the shapes of the Celtic underclass. Here they tie in to Joyce. Clairvoyance shifts into clarity. Kinsella and McCarthy become the prophetic but low-key stenographers of Dublin and Cork, tracing however gingerly the humiliation of their colonization and the shaming of their race. Their pain is not just this; it is also the long convalescence from these romantic obsessions. It is easy to be decisive like Yeats who didn't have to be haunted by his ancestors. What we have got here is, alongside the donkey of decay, the outline of a maturing Pegasus, a 'recovering' Ireland. The presence of rekindled emerald ashes leads to black spurts of outrage as well as ideological praise poems. In general, Kinsella stalks the first parameter, McCarthy the second.

The intimacy of politics is the lack of cosiness with history. Thomas McCarthy has been the sole full-time mystic of Dáil Éireann since Independence, ascribing revelation to the 1916 proclamation of the Republic and sacramentality to the Fianna Fáil party of De Valera and Charles Haughey. For him this sometimes majority party has been the assembly of the people. From Fianna Fáil come the stewards of the green acres. Kinsella too has stayed in the tradition of his father; the labour voice mostly though not totally represented in the Labour Party, the dark horse of the Republic which has never quite seen electoral legitimacy. Two riders: of a green Pegasus and a stars and a plough Pegasus. Note the separate treatments of the above two chieftains, the heraldic De Valera and the De Medici Haughey. In a country as politically claustrophobic as the 26 county Republic, the comparison between the writers' sympathies for varying charismas will be significant.

Let me first present the McCarthy recognition. First, the primal urge, the inheritance of the true Tone and forgiven O'Connell merged in De Valera:

My father recited prayers of memory,
Of monster meetings, blazing tar-barrels
Planted outside Free State homes, the Broy-

Harriers pushing through a crowd, Blueshirts;
And, after the war, De Valera's words
Making Churchill's imperial palette blur.

This is the partisan moment and the national moment fused; De Valera's funeral evokes the post-Táin nostalgia. Alas for McCarthy, but perhaps not for his poetry, the grandeur has ebbed to the long intricate scandal of Haughey: the 1932 green shamrock has lost its glitter. Flagging fortunes register on the Taoiseach's appearance and are captured on television:

The Taoiseach's face comes into grey focus
Like the lately usurped Turin Shroud.
His speech is barely audible. The distress
Of failure cannot he hidden from the crowd.

The Turin Shroud is a curious metaphor and might strike an observer as that of a De Valera redivivus looking into the patria of his heart, but it represents undoubtedly an end point or at the least a giant pause on this political road. How cool and ceremonious is Kinsella by contrast:

Upright, stately and blind, and hesitating
    solitary on the lavatory floor
after The Government meeting down the hall.
    De Valera. The last.

In my view this brief poem, which commemorates Jack Yeats as well as the head of Government, is elegant and connected. The artist hero and the warrior hero undergo transformation into golden memorials. Kinsella is hot and cold by turn for, as we shall see, his eye on Haughey resembles the savage bardic one. The Shroud of Turin is pelted with heavy stones!

Modifications of a neutral, if not benign, view of De Valera prevail in Kinsella's earlier poems. For pointed comment one could turn to a section of 'Nightwalker' which offers a vivid account of the manipulations of De Valera in the civil war, and in the section entitled 'Look the wedding group ...' the cast for betrayal is formed. The poem is based on a reading of Kevin O'Higgins's wedding photograph. The best man, Rory O'Connor, was executed by the Free State a few years later when O'Higgins was Minister for Justice and Ernest Blythe was a member of the cabinet. The groom was assassinated in 1928 in retaliation for the execution of the best man. All these events were set in motion by the civil war which in large part resulted from the refusal of De Valera, Rory O'Connor, and their allies, to accept the treaty with Great Britain that was passed on a Dáil vote:

> Enmity sprang up between them, and the Fox
> Took to the wilds. Then, to the Groom's sorrow,
> His dear friend left him also, vowing hatred.
> So they began destroying the groom's substance
> And he sent out to hunt the Fox, but trapped
> His friend instead; mourning, he slaughtered him.
> Shortly, in his turn the Groom was savaged
> On a Sunday morning, no one knows by whom.
> ....
> – A tragicomical tale:
> how the Fox, long after,
> Found a golden instrument one day,
> A great complex gold horn, left at his door;
> ....
> And gave it with dull humour to his old enemy
> The Weasel – who recognized the horn
> Of the Player King, and bared his needle teeth.

It is clear that in addition to O'Higgins and O'Connor the Fox is De Valera and the Weasel Blythe. Kinsella's nice touch makes W.B. Yeats the Player King and the Abbey Theatre the Golden Horn. The fratricidal neurosis of the years 1921–1923 is fulminated in Biblical terms. Kinsella establishes himself as a master in a tradition obtaining from Gaelic poets of the early modern period, the savage allegory. His ferocious precision here is reminiscent of Sean Ó Riordáin, his rival in stature.

Chief follows chief and in the next part of Kinsella's sequence the satiric gaze is concentrated on Haughey. The major element of the vituperative style here is Dantesque, reinforced by the geography of Stephen Dedalus and his dark tower:

> Fathers of Authors!
> It is himself! In silk hat and jowls
> Accoutred in stern jodhpurs! The sonhusband
> Coming in his power: mounting to glory
> On his big white harse [*sic*]!

All exclamation points underlining the derisive apocalyptic of 'Coming to power', the son not being Dedalus nor Christ but Sean Lemass's (De Valera's successor) son-in-law, the grisly 'sonhusband'. The term 'Nightwalker' has been analysed critically but despite its surface meanings I would hold that 'night' is the state of the corrupt and forsaken Republic, the 'night' when nationalism, with its concomitant worker and labour axis, turns finally sour. The ghost of Stephen Dedalus walking the area can only suggest, I told you so. It is almost an Elizabethan Nightwood where the promenader begins to roam and the Celtic sibyl sets herself to hiss. The doom foreseen appears in silk hat: Joyce's gombeen and Yeats's Paudeen, dressed to kill.

The colder eye is demonstratively Kinsella's and in political poetry this seems an advantage. In terms of working class ethos, Kinsella is the steelier, though McCarthy has written powerfully in this context. The Dublin poet places himself adroitly in empathy with his father and grandfather who both held employment in Guinness. Kinsella, reflecting on their working conditions, enjoys the power of latter-day rage. McCarthy's finest poem, in this environment, concerns himself in service to the Jamesons, the distillery family. The poet insinuates into his work record the racial curse The Republic was dreamt up to extinguish. Most of McCarthy's poems about occupations, leaving aside the ateliers of Paris, refer to his father campaigning for Fianna Fáil – what emerges from 'A July Afternoon on Jameson's Farm' sounds like clear slave revolt:

We are the small bearachs in
this life who come to earn their keep
with little hands and plastic cups,
who chafe their white Catholic skins
and mutter insults at each bush
that unleashes a clump of nettles.

One would need to quote the whole poem to savour the pageantry of its venom. Or one could quote the note to the poem: 'bearachs: migrant workers brought into Waterford from West Cork by Protestant colonists in the seventeenth century'. I admire the mix of idealism and vengeance and yet I adhere more happily to a working class context poem like Kinsella's 'Dick King' which somehow has under consideration more of the tonal realities and less of the dream. The Larkinite speaks to me more strongly than the bearach, though I must note there is more of the world outside Ireland in McCarthy.

A former world-wide generation spent considerable energy in searching for the perfect working class poem and poet. Some, in England, ordained D.H. Lawrence; others regretted the temporary nature of the Fabian hold on Auden, Spender, and Day Lewis. If I had to name the most competent poet at describing the monotony and sweat of toil I would choose Hopkins, in poems like 'Harry Ploughman', which suggests a sculpture of back-breaking serfdom and catches a blazing close-up quality. That it is like a camera shot enhances its veracity; it has none of the distant feeling of Wordsworth's peasants who seem to have a Potemkin orchestration. The quality one should look for in writing about workers seems best defined in a passage of Sherwood Anderson about Southern mill hands on strike:

> There is a way in which people, workers, when they are on strike, even when they are pretty sure to lose, get something … for a time at least, they get a rather fine feeling of each other … Hands reach out … Why, they are people in love … (quoted in Howe 217).

The study of the dispossessed, a concept popularized by Kinsella in a major anthology of Gaelic poetry of the penal centuries, can be examined for tribal loyalties under colonialism and for creative tension in relation to class and social justice. Perhaps it could also be looked at for evidence of partially changed minds. Both poets explore how disadvantaged sections of the Irish community were assumed into the setting up of the new state and its subsequent literature. The huge matter of emigration must also be figured in, but dispossession came before diaspora. This poetry judges these bondings and abandonments, with McCarthy working the rural areas and Kinsella profiling the city. Both poetries bring back the debate to concern about the ingrained Celtic structure of Chieftaincy. Taoiseachs have an almost hereditary role in this volatile and voluble small democracy. The writing we have partly surveyed shows that the post-colonial 'fix' is not benign, in at least the Republic.

These are radical voices hidden in the making of an independent state. The dissolution of poverty of mind is both a slow process and a slow relief. When we think of such poverty we think of the world that surrounded Stephen Dedalus, the sad product of unfulfilled Dublin. I add the sound of Thomas Kinsella and Thomas McCarthy to the music of Stephen Dedalus who found his Republic in 1904. What Hugh Kenner remarked about Kinsella is true also of McCarthy: 'For that is how it is in the world of these poems: nothing we might expect will be provided' (591). That is, if we had not been prepared by history and Joyce to anticipate the unexpected. Readers of this most intriguing Irish writing must keep their ears close to the breaking ground.

– from *Nua: Studies in Contemporary Irish Writing* (2002)

WORKS CITED

Howe, Irving. *Sherwood Anderson* (New York: Sloane Associates, 1951).

Kenner, Hugh. 'Thomas Kinsella: An Anecdote and Some Reflections', *Genre* 12, no. 4 (Winter 1979), 591.

Kinsella, Thomas. *Poems, 1956–1971* (Winston-Salem, NC: Wake Forest University Press, 1979).

Poems from City Centre (Dublin: The Dolmen Press, 1990). [Check this ref]

McCarthy, Thomas. *The First Convention* (Dublin: The Dolmen Press, 1978).

The Lost Province (London: The Anvil Press, 1996).

Seven Winters in Paris (London: The Anvil Press, 1989).

O'Hara, Daniel. 'Appropriate Performance: Thomas Kinsella and the Ordeal of Understanding', *Notes from the Land of the Dead*. Eds. James D. Brophy and Raymond J. Porter (Boston: Iona College Press, 1982).

Yeats, W.B. *The Collected Poems* (New York, Macmillan, 1952).

VOICES IN THE IRISH CITIES OF THE DEAD: MELODRAMA AND DISSENT IN FRANK MCGUINNESS'S *CARTHAGINIANS*

Carthaginians is an extraordinary challenge to, and fruition of, those shifting grounds of national identity which have produced a confident and even aggressive Irish theatre. It seems a natural irony that this century should bow out, *inter alia,* with McGuinness's work, a brilliant fireworks that illuminates the tenor of Wilde's and then Yeats's art suppositions. *Carthaginians* sets out with ferocity to dismember, and remember, the primary myth of a perpetual Catholic state of being, just as the companion piece *Observe the Sons of Ulster Marching Towards the Somme* does with its Protestant counterpart. *Carthaginians* is prickly and tangled, as well as it might be with its dispossessed subject. It also grapples with the sense of self within the tribe (McGuinness's own group), a decentred or 'bypath' self, and one that is often strikingly indeterminate.

The play limbers back to the concept that the doyen of the emerging Irish theatre, Lady Gregory, ceaselessly defined: that our art must be native, must allow itself, or lose itself, into becoming the Book of the People. But, unlike the panache of the Renaissance, it is a devolutionary process from the pastoral ideals of a 'Golden Age'. A major focus of the play is a subversion of the 'hedgeschool' tradition of Irish culture which compared Irish experience to that of Athens and Rome. McGuinness conceals his nostalgia. The basis of McGuinness's affray is a battle-scoured account of the common Catholic folk of Derry in their near-contemporary straits of distress. Their stories embody the Virgilian narrative of Dido and Aeneas which is united with the historical destruction of Carthage by Rome/Derry by the British army in the same way as *Ulysses* ties the paths of Stephen Dedalus and Bloom to the journeys of the *Odyssey*. McGuinness leaves no stone unturned to locate the cultural Irish corpse. This is helped by the great echo within the play of the schoolmaster Hugh's final words in Friel's *Translations*, 'Urbs antiqua fuit – there was an ancient city ...' (from Book I of Virgil's *Aeneid*). McGuinness performs its reinterment and resurrection. Over all, *Carthaginians* celebrates the mediaeval comic sense of a culture tragically frozen in a permanent 'present'. The playwright is both undertaker and priest who buries and then baptises. The structure of the play, always in dissolution, always between death and life, moves within the polarities of a liturgical week which must represent Holy Week, its prayers fuelled by its epigraph from Milosz: 'It is possible that there is no other memory than the memory of wounds'.

We must go then, classically, *in medias res*, to the table of contents built on Northern Ireland sand, following the hotchpotch of its dissident assumptions, capturing its melodramatic hysteria of quick fix and bottomless hole. The text uses the location phrase 'burial ground' instead of 'cemetery' for greater emphasis on the living; the seven characters (the author suggests there should be a maximum of seven graves to accompany them) stay there or come there for large blocks of hyper-catechetical activity. Everyone catechises in the text, especially the males; this may be a reflection of priesthood, but in any case it follows the primer of the Irish conversation: when not even in doubt, proceed by question and answer. Faith is thus administered and this quality the characters have, except they are without hope. They elaborate rituals in order to trash them; the catechism vanishes into the quiz or trivia show, especially the bar kind so popular in Ireland – a parlour game in which some answers may roll the stones from the tombs. McGuinness presents the quiz as the continuing examination of life just as the catechism reads as the scrutiny of God. We get the sense, from the former, of the endlessness of living history in popular culture, while the real question about purpose is postponed, the visionary context: will the dead arise, specifically will Maela's daughter rise? Will Derry rise again in justice?

The questions and answers shower like arrows, not like confetti. They circle, reform, and come again and again:

> PAUL: Who wrote *The Aeneid*? Virgil. Who did Virgil guide through the city of hell? That's a tough one, boys. Who will guide me through this city of hell?

Who wrote *Carthaginians*? Frank McGuinness. Who does Frank McGuinness guide through the city of hell? The collapsed city of Derry? The reader, the audience? But who did Virgil guide? Dante. So Dante stands for the resurrection-quest characters: Maela, Greta, Sarah, Dido, Hark, Paul, Seph (the names confer the Bible and art on the birth certificates of Derry). In classical epic the protagonists go to hell: Eurydice, Orpheus, Odysseus, Aeneas. At hell's gate the consequences of fate are discovered. Speech may be constructed that was impossible above ground. Now, though, hell is overground, a terrain of bombed sites and bombed-out people. The Northern Irish 'war' seems our end of the century, as Simone Weil writes on *The Iliad*:

> Once the experience of war makes visible the possibility of death that lies locked up in each moment, our thoughts cannot travel from one day to the next without meeting death's face.

One of the quiz questions concerns Antony and Cleopatra – an aftershadowing of another great romantic couple, another Mediterranean David and Wally, Aeneas and Dido, who moved in a mist of fine Latin metre, and are now reduced to pub argot. They move between two ruined port cities, from a queen who throws herself on the pyre to a queen who crossdresses:

> PAUL: Easy one. Which queen of Carthage ruled there until deserted by Aeneas?
> DIDO: Dido, Queen of Carthage.
> HARK: Dido, Queen of Derry.
> DIDO: At least I admit it, sunshine.

Another question poses the end of ambiguity and the start of return:

> PAUL: Hark's team, what does Carthage mean?
> *(They confer)*
> HARK: We dont know.
> DIDO: It means new city.
> PAUL: Correct.

Which delivers the illumination that Cato's famous message to the Roman Senate will be reversed. Carthage must be destroyed – now Carthage must be raised. New city, no longer Roman / British. The British have destroyed Londonderry; it must be raised, relived in, as Derry, new human city:

> PAUL: Good. Who wrote *The Aeneid*? An Irishman wrote. That's your only clue.

(Frank McGuinness wrote it?) Why is Virgil an Irishman? Because he is a poet who has seen hell, because he writes about empire and ruin, because he writes about a city rising from the Dead. In contrast to *Translations* which sees that 'city' dying, *Carthaginians* begins in a cemetery where the people roll the headstones back from themselves, where the epitaphs read out for the victims (of Bloody Sunday) dissolve into new writing. A metropolis of survival. A community still living in the ruins, yet having completed its liturgy of elegy, having mourned and examined the birds, Roman auguries that appear in the first scene. Part of the 'watch it' plan is the sense of the sacred in the task, exemplified by silence, the choice of music, the contour of a week that ends with salvation at midnight on Sunday. Each scene possibly stands in for a stage of Holy Week and the Passion of Jesus Christ until the chant of deliverance:

> PAUL: Is it after twelve?
> MAELA: Sunday.
> GRETA: Sunday.
> SARAH: Sunday.
> *(The women start to place the guns, balaclavas, and religious images on the sheet).*
> GRETA: Wash the dead.
> PAUL: Sunday.
> MAELA: Bury the dead.
> SEPH: Sunday.
> SARAH: Raise the dead.
> HARK: Sunday.
> DIDO: Did you see the dead?
> GRETA: The dead beside you.
> SEPH: Sunday.
> MAELA: The dead behind you.
> PAUL: Sunday.
> SARAH: The dead before you.
> SEPH: Change.
> PAUL: Changed.

In my estimation satire in this play is partly 'fruitful prayer'. Satire here includes as a major element parody, and in-jokes as a strand. The work of rebirth could not be just sweet salvation. It must contain its admittedly fragile stability and anarchist swings of mood and language and indeterminate identity, gender, history, and religion. McGuinness wisely mixes a broth here, finding melodrama useful to level and dissent instrumental in tough but hilarious reconstruction. An Irish audience must find laughter, otherwise it cannot engage in purgation. McGuinness, too, relies on the history of the theatre since the Literary Renaissance to justify his bludgeoning: 'One of the major assets you have as an Irish writer is that when an Irish audience comes to the theatre they are a play from Synge onwards ... A sense of the innate theatricality of life, so that an Irish audience will accept very willingly a play-within-a-play'. Before he arrives at such a prize, McGuinness puts more spin on the technique of the quiz that unravels disintegration. If Carthage was knocked first and then rebuilt – so must the foundations of the Irish Dramatic Movement. The target practice must commence with Yeats and the writers of the Revival who were themselves ambiguously Nationalist, capable of flirtation with violence (and might Friel be included here in some hidden agenda?). McGuinness, like any Irish writer, walks in a battle all over again, looking for an exit sign from the terms of the tenured Easter 1916 debate. We have been locked into Yeats so much, and his heirs O'Casey and Behan, that McGuinness looks for relief, light and otherwise. The setting for this version of non-pastoral is as far away as possible from the drawing room:

> HARK: Not the Derry Renaissance?
> PAUL: Where else, big fella?
> DIDO: What Derry Renaissance?
> HARK: The Derry Renaissance was strictly confined to pubs. Correction, one pub.

Echo might treat it like this: What Literary Renaissance? The Irish Literary Renaissance. Where did it take place? It was strictly confined to 'At-homes'. Correction, one 'at-home'. Which one? Mr. Yeats of Merrion Square, blockhead ...'

The most flagellating ritual in *Carthaginians* is performed by Dido and the whole cast in the play-within-the-play, 'The Burning Balaclava', by Fionnuala McGonigle (in itself a take-off of one of Yeats's occult writer friends in the nineties who was hermaphroditic). The cast play characters of the opposite sex in this exquisite burlesque with the sectarian roles reversed and with obvious but scintillating parodies of O'Casey (*Juno and the Paycock*), Behan (*The Hostage*), Shakespeare, and even *West Side Story*. 'The Burning Balaclava' is a vaudeville re-enactment of Bloody Sunday, down to McGuinness having the priest waving white sheets (borrowed from the reality of the heroism of Bishop Daly on that occasion – also a figure used by Brian Friel in *Freedom of the City*). This ludicrous playlet affords the characters the moment to face their nightmares, to move beyond death-like coldness and repression. Like the lepers in the New Testament, they do not thank their liberator, Dido, for allowing the blood of that Sunday (Passion Sunday?) to be washed away. However, this is the imitation of reconciliation. Maela accepts that her daughter is dead, Seph has the ability to speak as he confesses his sin of informing; all of them can litanise Derry's dead together. Dido emerges as high priest, who can hear ever more extraordinary confessions. Perhaps he is a kind of contextual bishop (remember, St Augustine was bishop of Hippo, that is, Carthage). Is this climax-within-climax the equivalent of Maundy Thursday, when Jesus washes the feet of the disciples? It is hard to be definite but the point remains: deliverance occurred by some collective sublimation of parody.

And where does that gift come from, or where does it go back to? The grace of such survival is evidently Wildean. Dido performs the role of the catalyst: the artist in Wilde's language. In fact, the wit and wisdom of Wilde on sex, faith, politics, is the bright glue of *Carthaginians*. We first see it in the throw-away wit of the early scenes where Dido can fall into the fusillades of Wilde's comedies. There is, however, a serious vein in McGuinness that mixes fun with ideology. Richard Pine, in his *Irish Literary Supplement* profile of McGuinness, quotes him as saying:

> *The Soul of Man under Socialism* is a genuine attempt to cause havoc and to take a playful attitude to politics, which is a very healthy way of the writer and politics meeting.

McGuinness's work as a whole reflects and draws attention to Wilde's aesthetics, art and fun with the psalms of tears. Dido is the constructed personality alive to all the nuances of suffering, a working-class version of the Baudelairean 'Artist of Life'. I think of this queen of Derry being a more 'advanced' character than any Wilde figure, perhaps a Salome with a social conscience. Oscar is an ancestor and the times have moved on. Friel and McGuinness dare more than Wilde was able to (though that giant had the mind and means to do so). McGuinness's Christ in Dido and the other saints of *Carthaginians* are not hazy; this Christ works harder. Perhaps it is safe to say Wilde leans on Jesus, especially in *De Profundis* and *Reading Gaol*; Dido and the others momentarily absorb him. Yet when we shift to the end of *Carthaginians*, we have Wilde's tears on our faces.

We are watching the Dido of compassion, the pioneer of love and cheer to the living dead in the cemetery. Dido is the first to triumph over his memories, over revenge. Dido's physical and verbal acts of defiance establish the parameters of liberation. The ultimate voice in *Carthaginians* resembles perhaps that of Simone Weil. Consider her description of the pure soul opposed to the wantonness of the conqueror in *The Iliad*: 'The soul that wakes then, to live for an instant only to be lost almost at once in force's vast kingdom, awakes pure and whole ...' Dido enacts the Veronica figure when he wipes the sausage off Hark's face. As he does this, we come to the most didactic incident in the play. Dido tells of the day he was given his name by a Lebanese sailor (the Phoenicians from Lebanon became the Carthaginians!):

MAELA: What was he doing in Derry?

DIDO: Wandering through like myself. When he gave me the flowers I was sure I'd scored and then he put his hand to my face and I thought yipee but he just knelt down on the ground like this. (*Kneels*) He said, "Listen, listen, to the earth. The earth can speak. It says, 'Cease, cease your violent hand, for I am the earth and I accept my dead but I will no longer accept your dead, given to me by your violent hand. I am a peaceful earth, give me not your dead'".

This is the message from the Mother Goddess: Send me no corpses from the war. Throw no more victims into this bog. Wash the dead, see there are no more dead, watch it, survive, love your neighbour, say your own prayers. McGuinness, in his *Irish Times* 'Reflections on the Decade', adds:

> The greatest mistake we have made is not that we didn't love our neighbour, rather that we don't know them, and that is our continued, mutual choice. May we be forgiven, but I hope we won't be, since we forgive for all the wrong reasons. There is still so much to learn. Who from? Listen to Oscar Wilde, the prophet of the last Nineties.

– from *Irish University Review* (1995)

THREE

Interview with James Liddy

Michael S. Begnal

MIKE BEGNAL: The questions are going to sound rather silly and formal now probably, without the alcohol. But I just wanted to start by ...

JAMES LIDDY: Let's pretend we're still drunk.

MIKE BEGNAL: Okay.

JAMES LIDDY: It's on, yeah?

MIKE BEGNAL: It's on. Yeah.

JAMES LIDDY: Right.

MIKE BEGNAL: ... By mentioning your association with Kavanagh. Sometimes it seems that there's sort of a blackness to Kavanagh's work whereas yours is more celebratory. Yet you're such a big Kavanagh guy. Where would you see the link in terms of the work?

JAMES LIDDY: Well, his later work is especially redemptive; the canal bank poems in the last section of his *Collected Poems* seem to me to be visionary and accepting, and to have the immanence of God in the universe. But there, of course, are differences. First of all, I always envied Kavanagh having a farmer's background. And that was reality, the life of the farm, the enclosed life of the family, like monks in the house. Whereas I had the middle-class life of a doctor's son, not involved with the realities of the fields or the street even. And so he had that background of experience, and perhaps suffering, or at least that privilege, in an educational sense. And so that makes his poetry very strong, makes my poetry a little weaker. But the self-indulgence of my poems would come really from my own background. Not to be a Marxist or anything, but if you are relieved from stress when you're young by a nice background it doesn't necessarily prepare you to write about what exists or what's real, or what you should write about. Kavanagh is superior to me in that respect, and perhaps also in that he had that note of authority, which was possible to exercise in those days. The kind of prophetic, or at least big, authority coming from being a great writer. Perhaps also, from the Irish background, a note of spiritual prophesy. But by the time I came along, that was all suspect, or impossible.

MIKE BEGNAL: Brian Arkins [author of *James Liddy: A Critical Study*] makes much of the bohemianism in your work. We were talking about this last night – in Ireland 'bohemian' sometimes seems to be a dirty word.

JAMES LIDDY: Not in the Ireland I used to live in. People were envious of our wild style of living. Envious of the fact that we had the money to be able to buy drinks all day at McDaid's. And some of us had even got cars. And so the idea of 'bohemian' being a dirty word, it doesn't come from an Ireland I know. I would think that when I was young, 'bohemia' was a section of Dublin that was well-known though but obscure to most Dubliners, and I think in the countryside the concept 'bohemia' was considered the lives of the artists and the lives of the poor émigrés over in Paris. And it comes from 'wine, women, and song'. The turn against bohemianism I don't understand, except as a rigid morality that has come in. Queen Victoria has returned to this island and is imposing her moral standards on people.

MIKE BEGNAL: Yes. I suppose this sort of leads into the other questions to do with your love of Kerouac. And the fact that Kerouac has never been understood in Ireland. How would you say that American writers like Kerouac, and the Beats and so on, have shaped the course of your own writing.

JAMES LIDDY: Well, I knew the Beats before I ever went to the United States. All the City Lights Books were sold at Hodges Figgis on Dawson Street, the little pocket books. I read *Howl*, I read the … [*James is informed that he has a phone call and the tape is briefly stopped*].

MIKE BEGNAL: You were talking about Kerouac and the beats, and how you got their books at Hodges Figgis.

JAMES LIDDY: I should say more about that. I was attracted to Ginsberg I think even before Kerouac, because he was a poet. And because perhaps his vision of love was more communicable to me. I read Kerouac at the same time too, but it's always easier for me to read poetry. So Ginsberg first and Kerouac second. They became part of my mind. They were as influential as Kavanagh and Yeats, and other non-Irish poets. What they did for me was to give me a balance to Ireland, and also to bring in a new kind of – as much as the word 'spirituality' is nice it's overused – a new kind of awareness, and a new kind of consciousness about being a poet. And also about being, perhaps, a lover. Or perhaps about the soul of a lover or the soul of a poet, about [*what*] the basic concentration inside such a person would be. And it satisfied my thirst for the sublime. And Lorca, for the connection between Whitman, Lorca, and Ginsberg. There's that chain of sort of homoerotic poetry. There's all this sublime, high articulation [*which*] was an immense influence on me. Now Kerouac is somewhat different. I think he was like Kavanagh. He celebrated the mundane, the everyday. And he put the everyday into some extraordinary sentences. He was able to convey poetically the ordinariness of everything, which I thought Kavanagh did. And so I think that Kerouac was a second Kavanagh, to me. And I think that they style, the writing style, was liberation. That you could move more freely, with spontaneous writing, and not just interior monologue.

MIKE BEGNAL: 'Spontaneous' is another dirty word in Ireland.

JAMES LIDDY: I know. Well, take comfort. All the dirty words in Ireland are holy words in the cosmos. And – it was very much in a way a kind of monologue or description, in a kind of inspirational way, and if you could do that ... I mean, that's difficult to do, but if you could do that, like Kerouac was able to do it so well, with the language resources he had ...

MIKE BEGNAL: That's the thing. If you aren't as good as that, spontaneous sometimes doesn't work.

JAMES LIDDY: Sometimes spontaneous only works for those whom the muse, the imagination, permits it to work. If you don't mind me saying so, it's a heavenly influence. And if you have that, you have everything, you can speak as spontaneous as you like. Very few people are gifted like that. I wouldn't know whether to say I was spontaneous, but I have elements of spontaneity. But it wouldn't be of the style of Kerouac, because Kerouac also was less spontaneous, there were scenes that he would revise ...

MIKE BEGNAL: Oh, of course, yeah.

JAMES LIDDY: But he was very given to the first draft, and I think that there's a great truth to the first draft. Not always publishable, but editable. The truth can be edited.

MIKE BEGNAL: You're also often very autobiographical, the way that Kerouac and other Beats were.

JAMES LIDDY: Well, of course. It's about me – beautiful, gorgeous, manic-depressed, dying me. And that's one of the most extraordinary subjects in the world. Everyone has that ego waiting to be adorned.

MIKE BEGNAL: How do you think that would read on paper if someone were to read that, 'It's all about me?'

JAMES LIDDY: Yes, it's all about me, but it's all about me in a very interesting way. Well it has to be about me, it has to be about the others, it has to be about you, and the rest of the world. And it's about me, basically childhood and early dreams, about parents, first education and all that. But it also has to be who you are in the world, meeting people. I've met writers because I knew where they drank, and I was able to drink. So it was about me, but it was about them, and it was about us. And I think that you can carry that on. The idea in Richard Murphy's memoirs is that he translates diary entries into autobiographical prose. There's certain remove, and certain looking back, and a certain wryness, maybe nostalgia. I would never write like that. I would never keep a diary or a journal. I know the Beats kept journals, but that's an American industrial habit. The Irish are too busy talking to keep journals, they're too busy drinking. It's a lie to write them down. But they do have inside themselves an archive. It's your own archive, you know. Kavanagh himself wrote memoirs, you know. *Tarry Flynn* is a memoir, in a sense, a childhood memoir.

MIKE BEGNAL: Is there any distance in your poems?

JAMES LIDDY: Well, you have to clarify the word 'distance'.

MIKE BEGNAL: You know, it's not just straight autobiography. In the sense of this being a poem as well.

JAMES LIDDY: Well, it's a piece of writing, and you have to uses sound, resonance, syntax. Imagination has to hover over it. It has to be decorated, but not over-decorated. It has to seek memory, but it has to also prod memory. It has to create the actuality. I think my days at the temple of the muses was a sort of utopia. I mean a flawed and dangerous utopia, but a utopia nonetheless. And also, I think about early friendships, [*which*] were an addition to utopia, to utopian romantic friendship. And all of that, you know, comes from before the early sections of the autobiography, and then later on some more adult – let's just say I later grew up – the more adult experiences in the United States. It's a big country to grow up in, but you don't grow up too much because it's a Romantic country.

MIKE BEGNAL: That sort of leads to my next question. You also mentioned that Kerouac provided a sort of counter-balance to Ireland, and of course you have this whole American aspect to your life and your work.

JAMES LIDDY: My mother was an American ...

MIKE BEGNAL: How does this duality sit with you?

JAMES LIDDY: Well, I don't know, that's a difficult question. I couldn't be glib about the answer to this question. I feel absolutely, indubitably Irish. And I feel of an Ireland of a certain earlier period, and a non-nationalist Ireland – but I was a nationalist when I was young. As regards to what America does, I think it provides the escape from Ireland. It's the emigration thing. You're bringing your country with you, inside you, inside your mind – bring it over there! – and reassembling it, you know. I think that the distance is the distance of the Atlantic Ocean, and it's also the distance you have from your past as you grow older. You have a strong past, but you also have a different perspective on it. There's immense distance there. But the American part – what is America? America is to the Irish writer, or should be, a form of liberation. Not just the Beat thing, but political liberation, and it was also the era of Civil Rights and so forth. And I think the Beat Generation in its day, and even in Ireland for me, was a rite of liberation, a passage of liberation. And you go to the country and you find all that in it. Now, forty or thirty years later, it doesn't seem so liberated.

MIKE BEGNAL: You translated Baudelaire.

JAMES LIDDY: Yeah.

MIKE BEGNAL: Do you think that translation, particularly in your case with translating Baudelaire, do you think that that has in a way enabled you to subsume something of Baudelaire into your own work?

JAMES LIDDY: Well, that's all a theory of correspondences. That Baudelaire had a bit of a hold on Edgar Allen Poe, that they never knew each other, but that they were somehow in tune, and their spirits or their psyches or whatever were able to migrate to each other's places and into each other's work. I thought myself that they shouldn't take influence to the front of the stage. You can take it into something like a correspondence with the other person. The sort of across-time-and-space relationship, based not just on language and writing, but based upon spirit. And I felt when I was translating Baudelaire that I *was* Baudelaire. I still feel that. I feel as [*close*] to Baudelaire that I can see clearly and plainly from a personal perspective, I can see him, as he was and as he wrote, that I can see it right in front of me what he was doing. I don't say he was identical to me, but I understand everything he did, I understand what his poems were about. And it's also that kind of decadent Catholicism, which has also appealed to me.

MIKE BEGNAL: Is Baudelaire as important as Kavanagh and Kerouac then for you?

JAMES LIDDY: Yeah, I think so. The Symbolists created modern literature, in many ways.

MIKE BEGNAL: Yeah, that's right.

JAMES LIDDY: France is the birthplace really of modern art, modern poetry. I think that the French have to be there. And it's not just Baudelaire, I mean you have Rimbaud and Mallarmé and so on, and others. So I think that Baudelaire could be an Irishman in some way, the European sense, and I also think in the Catholic sense, Baudelaire could've been, or should've been from Dublin. You can transpose him to Dublin, the Dublin that I knew. You could see Baudelaire in McDaid's.

MIKE BEGNAL: Do you think Clarence Mangan is something of a Baudelaire/Irish Baudelaire-type figure?

JAMES LIDDY: Yes he is, isn't he? He had the affinities with Poe as well. Baudelaire had a conscious affinity with him; [*he*] created the theory of correspondence. He translated Poe, of course, Baudelaire did. Now Mangan and Poe are almost of the same years, had almost the same addictions and almost the same misery. I like Mangan, I agree with James Joyce in his article about Mangan, and the poetry it sweeps along, there's a beautiful roll to it, an elegant lamentation. But it doesn't come to me like Baudelaire. I don't see Mangan, I don't know Mangan. I mean, I like his poems. I don't know him. I'm not there in him.

MIKE BEGNAL: We were talking a little bit about MacGreevy last night, Thomas MacGreevy.

JAMES LIDDY: Oh, Tom MacGreevy, yeah.

MIKE BEGNAL: Do you think he should be a little more widely read in Ireland than he is? How do you rate his importance in terms of Irish literature?

JAMES LIDDY: Well first of all, there's still too many poets, too many poets to make a literature. Too many cooks spoil the broth. The broth is thin. But on the other hand, there's an awful lot of soups on the menu. I think that MacGreevy is unfairly hidden amongst a crowd of poets. Now if we go back to his time, there weren't so many poets around. But he did it. Talk about distance, he kept an immense distance between himself and art. He seemed to me to be more Irish than anyone I'd ever met almost. Perhaps like Mangan. He had more Irish,

Celtic, nineteenth-century, small town, big city, Irishman in Paris, chevalier, soldier, emigrant – he had that quality. And there was a quality of distance. But that made for difficulties for writing poetry. I don't know why he only wrote one book. I guess he would have said that you don't have to write more than one book, or that you don't have to necessarily continue writing, what you have to do is serve God or Ireland or be a good friend. He wasn't totally committed to writing. Wasn't *engage,* even though he lived in Paris [*Laughs*].

MIKE BEGNAL: How do you see your own writing in relation to what's being done now, in Ireland first of all, and then more generally in the US or wherever? Do you have any connections with anyone in terms of literature?

JAMES LIDDY: Well, I know a number of poets. I know the older poets quite well, Montague and Kinsella. But obviously they're older than me slightly, and they … of course I met them when I was young, and absorbed them. And they created all that post-Kavanagh/post-Yeatsian literary Ireland for me. And I think it's substantial with Kinsella and Montague and others, in cases. I suppose that is a source of relationship between myself and a continuity with that. But Lar Cassidy, who died, told me that … once he said I was a modernist, and that Kinsella was a modernist poet, and Montague was a modernist poet, and we were the generation of modernism in Ireland. And that modernism came late, because it came perhaps in the Second World War, and in the 50s and 60s. And that's probably true. That is the true connection with international literature, I think maybe that's my relationship,

MIKE BEGNAL: Poets like Michael Smith and Trevor Joyce are known for being latter-day Irish modernists in a sense.

JAMES LIDDY: They came after me; they're younger than me. And they took up the poetry of the 30s, Devlin and Coffey and others. And took up MacGreevy. And they came to a sense of surrealism, via Niall Montgomery, and they had a kind of a connection like that. Theirs was somewhat, to me, a bibliographical connection. I suppose Michael Smith's connection was through editing these people and republishing them in *The Lace Curtain*. He was able to make a conscious connection, but almost as a formal annotation, or a postscript really.

MIKE BEGNAL: Are you sort of out there on your own, do you think? Do you have many readers in Ireland; do you have any influence?

JAMES LIDDY: Well, who knows? I mean, my name is known, and I've been publishing for many years and there have been reviews, though my last book didn't get reviewed in *The Irish Times*. I think there is some influence there. But I'm trying to be different; I'm trying to write in such a way that nobody else would write. And eventually … I think some people hear that. I wouldn't know, because a poet is hidden from his admirers, you know, you never meet these people. You never know who likes your poetry, you have no idea. Maybe very few people read it. You can't say. It's in the lap of the gods, you know. But one has to try to be different. That's the example of Baudelaire, and I think one must always be different.

MIKE BEGNAL: Yes, Um, Brian Arkins said that *Gold Set Dancing* is your *summa*.

JAMES LIDDY: *Summa Theologica …*

MIKE BEGNAL: If that is your *summa*, what do you do after your *summa*?

JAMES LIDDY: Well then I become a '*post summa*' [*Laughs*].

MIKE BEGNAL: Yeah …

JAMES LIDDY: Well, I think that's a nice catchy phrase. Arkins' book on me is honourable and intelligent, and leans in a certain direction, and that's all right and I wish the Holy Ghost upon his great spirit. But I don't think that really means anything, the '*summa*'. You have to wait till the end, the party's not over!

MIKE BEGNAL: Yeah, that's too tidy really.

JAMES LIDDY: It is, and also one has unpublished work, that I don't find needs to be published, and one has lots of continuities and stuff, and one has to edit what one hasn't published. But there's a lot left out. So I think Arkins thinks, writing as a scholar, that my work consists of what I have published. But I hold, as a poet, that a lot of my work consists of what I haven't published. So there's no *summa.*

– from *The Burning Bush* (2002)

Reader's Notes

READER'S NOTES

Reader's Notes